W9-BRZ-534

The Elements of Mentoring

JESSAMINE COUNTY PUBLIC LIBRARY
600 South Main Street
Nicholasville, KY 40356
(859) 885-3523

The
Elements
of
Mentoring

W. Brad Johnson and Charles R. Ridley

palgrave
macmillan

3 2530 60578 6928

THE ELEMENTS OF MENTORING
Copyright © W. Brad Johnson and Charles R. Ridley, 2004.
All rights reserved. No part of this book may be used or reproduced in
any manner whatsoever without written permission except in the case of
brief quotations embodied in critical articles or reviews.

First published 2004 by
PALGRAVE MACMILLAN™
175 Fifth Avenue, New York, N.Y. 10010 and
Houndmills, Basingstoke, Hampshire, England RG21 6XS.
Companies and representatives throughout the world.

PALGRAVE MACMILLAN is the global academic imprint of the
Palgrave Macmillan division of St. Martin's Press, LLC and of Palgrave
Macmillan Ltd. Macmillan® is a registered trademark in the United
States, United Kingdom and other countries. Palgrave is a registered
trademark in the European Union and other countries.

ISBN 1–4039–6401–7 hardcover

Library of Congress Cataloging-in-Publication Data
Johnson, W. Brad.
The elements of mentoring / W. Brad Johnson, Charles R. Ridley.
   p. cm.
  Includes bibliographical references and index.
  ISBN 1–4039–6401–7
  1. Mentoring in business. 2. Mentoring in the professions.
3. Mentoring in education. 4. Employees—Counseling of.
5. Mentoring. I. Ridley, Charles R. II. Title.

HF5385.J64 2004
658.3'124—dc22   2003060923

658.3124
John

A catalogue record for this book is available from the British Library.

Design by Letra Libre, Inc.

First edition: April 2004
10 9 8 7 6 5 4 3 2 1

Printed in the United States of America.

With love, gratitude, and endless admiration,
we dedicate this book to our children—
our greatest protégés—
Jacob, Daniel, and Stanton Johnson;
and Charles and Charliss Ridley

Contents

Acknowledgments

We thank Toby Wahl, acquisitions editor at Palgrave Macmillan, for finding promise in our idea and delivering encouragement at all the right times. We are further grateful to Donna Cherry, Meg Weaver, and the Palgrave production staff for bringing this work through all the important stages without a hitch.

I thank my wife, Laura Johnson, for her patience, love, and more patience. She brings grace, elegance, and endless kindness to a home full of guys. I am grateful to Erick Bacho, Marsha Beaugrand, Mark Eastburg, John Ralph, and Corky Vazquez—each of them colleagues and friends of the best sort. I am particularly indebted to my graduate school mentor, Charles R. Ridley, who embodies the elements of mentoring. His example piqued my ongoing interest in the power of good mentoring.

—W. B. J.

I thank Iris Ridley, my wife, who embodies a richness of love, self-sacrifice, and an endearing spirit. For my many protégés, I have been blessed to participate in their personal and professional pilgrimages. I especially thank Brad Johnson who is the consummate protégé and who encouraged me to develop my ideas on mentoring.

—C. R. R.

Preface

The reasonable thing is to learn from those who can teach.

—*Sophocles*

.

This is a short book, but not because there is little to say. Much has been written about the art and science of mentoring. In the last several years alone, thousands of books and journal articles have addressed the topic. There are research reports, narrative accounts, and manuals for professionals, spiritual leaders, and friends. In this book, we zero in on the basics and eliminate unnecessary words. Our goal is to untangle the morass of research and writing on the topic. We offer readers a clear summary of the fundamental principles of mentoring—principles we deem to be universal. We do this without fluff, hype, and myth. These are simply the nuts and bolts of being a good mentor—nothing more.

Our heroes in the world of pithy writing are William Strunk and E. B. White. In their now-classic *The Elements of Style,* Strunk and White offer crucial rules for avoiding basic mistakes in composition. Rule 17, *Omit Needless Words,* states: "Vigorous writing is concise. A sentence should contain no unnecessary words, a paragraph no unnecessary sentences, for the same reason that a drawing should have no unnecessary lines and a machine no unnecessary parts" (Strunk & White 2000, p. 23). In our view, a book on the crucial elements of mentoring should also contain nothing unnecessary. Our singular purpose is to distill the research-supported fundamentals on being an effective mentor.

In preparation for the writing of this book, we conducted an extensive search of the scholarly literature on mentoring and read more than a thousand publications from business, psychology, education, and other fields. We gave more weight to research studies and downplayed "feel-good" pieces on the topic. We searched for findings with direct relevance to mentors; we combed the research for data-supported truths about what makes a mentor excellent. In *The Elements of Mentoring*, we funnel the voluminous mentoring literature into a terse guide for the practicing mentor. The result is a short list of the essential ingredients of mentoring; what new mentors need to know and what seasoned mentors must occasionally remember. These are the "rules of engagement" for serious mentors. We introduce each element with an applied case study of excellent mentoring in practice. Each case study represents an amalgam of several good mentorships we have witnessed over the years. Although each case alone is fictitious, each is a clear example of the best mentoring practice. We conclude each element with a terse summary of its basic ingredients—the *key components*. In the trenches, readers may quickly refer back to these salient summaries of each crucial mentoring element. The elements of mentoring cut across all academic disciplines, professions, and contexts. They hold true for managers, professors, teachers, clinical supervisors, and anyone else committed to mentoring. These truths should be as compelling for teachers as for CEOs of multinational corporations.

Our own interest in mentoring stems from our extensive work with students, consulting clients, and research participants. We are licensed psychologists and college professors with a background of researching and writing about mentorships. Brad Johnson is a faculty member in both the Department of Leadership, Ethics, and Law at the U.S. Naval Academy and at the Graduate School of Business and Education at Johns Hopkins University. Charles Ridley is a professor of counseling psychology and associate dean in the Graduate School at Indiana University. He is also an organizational consultant. Both of us have written extensively and have mentored scores of excellent graduate students. We are also a mentor-protégé pair. Our own successful mentorship during Brad Johnson's graduate school career triggered an ongoing interest in the various facets of mentoring—particularly the elements of mentor excellence.

We have distilled the vast mentoring literature into 57 key elements for effective mentoring. The elements are clustered around six primary themes—what excellent mentors do (matters of skill); the traits of excellent mentors (matters of style and personality); arranging the mentor–protégé relationship (matters of beginning); knowing thyself as mentor (matters of integrity); when things go wrong (matters of restoration); and welcoming change and saying goodbye (matters of closure). We conclude with a list of important references. These sources are for professionals or scholars who wish to read the research and scholarly literature in greater detail.

Mentoring relationships (mentorships) are dynamic, reciprocal, personal relationships in which a more experienced person (mentor) acts as a guide, role model, teacher, and sponsor of a less experienced person (protégé). Mentors provide protégés with knowledge, advice, counsel, support, and opportunity in the protégé's pursuit of full membership in a particular profession. Outstanding mentors are intentional about the mentor role. They select protégés carefully, invest significant time and energy in getting to know their protégés, and deliberately offer the career and support functions most useful for their protégés. Mentoring is an act of generativity—a process of bringing into existence and passing on a professional legacy. In Homer's epic poem, *The Odyssey,* Mentor was an Ithacan noble and trusted friend of Odysseus. He was charged with caring for Odysseus's son Telemachus when Odysseus departed for the Trojan War. Later in the poem, the goddess Athena assumes Mentor's form to guide, protect, and teach Telemachus during his travels. In this role, Mentor (and Athena) serve as coach, teacher, guardian, protector, and kindly parent. Mentor shared wisdom, promoted Telemachus's career, and actively engaged him in a deep personal relationship.

Mentoring is more than a fad. It is a well-researched helping relationship. Mentoring is associated with positive personal and career outcomes. What are the outcomes of mentoring? First, research consistently demonstrates the following benefits for mentored protégés: enhanced promotion rates, higher salaries, accelerated career mobility, improved professional identity, greater professional competence, increased career satisfaction, greater acceptance within the organization, and decreased job stress and role conflict. Mentored individuals also are more likely to mentor others. Second, mentors themselves benefit through internal satisfaction and fulfillment, enhanced creativity and professional synergy, career and personal rejuvenation, development of a loyal support base, recognition by the organization for developing talent, and generativity (pleasure associated with shaping future generations). Finally, organizations reap tangible benefits. Supervisors and managers who mentor experience increased productivity, enhanced organizational commitment, decreased turnover, and accelerated development of in-house talent. And mentored employees are more likely to remain committed to the organization. It is apparent that competent mentoring has the potential for win-win outcomes for protégés, mentors, and the organizations they serve.

Whether you are a new supervisor or a seasoned mentor, we hope *The Elements of Mentoring* serves as an invaluable tool for developing and promoting junior talent. Our hope is that it will help to sharpen your edge, increase your self-confidence, and add an irreplaceable dimension of fulfillment and satisfaction to your life and career. We also hope you will share this tool with others.

W. Brad Johnson   Charles R. Ridley
Annapolis, Maryland   Bloomington, Indiana

The Elements of Mentoring

What Excellent Mentors Do

Matters of Skill

So what is a mentor supposed to *do* anyway? If this question has crossed your mind, you are not alone. Although some of us have benefited from the teaching and coaching of an excellent mentor (or two), many of us have never been mentored and might wonder how such a relationship should actually be structured. Specifically, we wonder what to *do* once a decision to mentor is made. In this section of *The Elements*, we focus on the tangible behaviors or *functions* of mentoring. Each of these functional mentoring elements requires a combination of knowledge, attitude, and skills. Knowledge is informed understanding. You should understand how each distinct mentoring element is crucial for your protégé's development and how you might most effectively deliver it in your unique context or professional field. Attitude is the perspective or point of view. Each mentoring component will be useful only if it is approached in the right spirit and exclusively for the benefit of the protégé. Skill is behavior designed to serve a specific purpose. Many of the elements we discuss require experience and seasoning to master. They must be deliberately strengthened and sharpened.

Some of the skill-based mentoring functions are designed primarily to facilitate a protégé's career development. At times, a mentor sponsors a protégé for a new position, coaches a protégé through the nuances of a new task, or gives a challenging assignment intended to stretch a protégé beyond his or her comfort zone. Here the mentor is demonstrating *career functions.* At other times, the mentor understands that the pro-tégé's emotional and personal development require attention and inter-vention. A mentor may give much needed affirmation, encourage the pursuit of dreams, lend emotional support, or engage in increasing col-legial friendship with the protégé. Here the mentor is demonstrating *psychosocial functions.*

Each of the 19 elements included in this section are matters of skill. Each can be learned. With the appropriate attitudes (a sincere and gen-erative interest in the growth of others; what we refer to as the *character virtue of care*) and necessary knowledge (something we hope *The Elements* helps you to achieve), we believe you have the prerequisites for mastering these mentoring functions. Also, keep in mind that these elements of mentoring are much like tools in the toolbox of a master mechanic. Dis-cretion is needed for the appropriate use of the tools. Skillful mechanics know that they cannot use all of their tools at one time, that some tools may be inappropriate for certain jobs, and that some tools are more im-portant than others. In a similar manner, mentors assess individual pro-tégés and determine which combination of elements is likely to be most helpful at each stage in a protégé's development. Overall, mentors need more than simply having the right tools in their toolboxes. They need to know how to use these tools to get good results.

1
Select Your Protégés Carefully

As a successful senior manager in a thriving electronics company, Steve fre-quently supervised and interacted with junior managers and managerial trainees. Although he was courteous, fair, and helpful in these relationships, Steve was cautious when it came to developing more in-depth mentorships. During a five-year period, he intentionally mentored three new managers—all of whom shared his interests in and commitment to the organization. Intentional men-toring requires deliberate and thoughtful planning. Steve was careful to consider a protégé's specific mentoring needs. Each of these protégés caught Steve's atten-tion through their stellar job performance, initiative, and frequent interaction. Although he had the reputation of being an excellent mentor, and although he was often approached by junior managers for career guidance, Steve was acutely conscious of his limited resources (e.g., time, energy, and opportunities for including protégés in his work). For this reason, he carefully scrutinized promising new managers, determined the level of chemistry or "match" in their interactions, and then firmly committed himself only to the small number he believed he could carefully and successfully assist through the early phase of their careers.

Choosing protégés is like investing. You have limited resources and expect good returns. Like stocks, bonds, and mutual funds, some investments are better than others. More importantly, some investments are better matched to your personal preferences, needs, and risk tolerance. Mentors must behave like prudent investors; they must be selective in their choice of protégés. Successful mentors are vigilant and discerning of the traits, talents, and interests of their junior personnel and careful to embark on mentorships only with those who match them well. The investment should pay dividends for both mentor and protégé.

There is another reason for being selective. You cannot mentor everyone. No matter how energized, idealistic, and gifted you are, taking on too many protégés is a sure way to compromise your own health and the quality of your mentoring. Excellent mentors appreciate the costs of mentoring. It takes time, emotional energy, and professional resources, and everyone certainly has limitations. But competent mentors can get trapped. Because of their recognized competence, they are often sought out for their services. Unless they set limits, they easily can become overwhelmed and set themselves up for negative outcomes.

What happens when a mentor fails at the task of selectivity? In attempting to mentor too many protégés, or protégés with whom he or she is poorly matched, the mentor dilutes the power of mentoring in the lives of protégés. The mentor also diminishes his or her own enjoyment of the mentoring experience, which ironically is perhaps the greatest benefit of being a mentor. The well-intended but over-extended mentor pays a price—sometimes to the extent of becoming exhausted, detached, emotionally muted, or even cynical toward his or her protégés. Excellent mentors know when to "say no." When they find themselves fully committed, they gracefully decline accepting new mentoring relationships, especially with poorly matched juniors. In so doing, they protect their current cadre of protégés from poor mentoring as well as help ensure their own vitality.

Look at the other side. What about the psychology of mentors who just can't say no? The obvious consequences are a failure to set limits, inadequate self-care, and ultimately, burnout. They are perpetually overextended—hurried and needlessly pressured as anyone would attest. But the causes are less apparent than the consequences. Failure to set limits may indicate poor assertiveness skills or fear of rejection. It might represent an unhealthy need for approval or an insatiable need to be needed. Being pursued by potential protégés might feed a mentor's need for importance or status. And failure to set limits could reflect a mentor's misunderstanding of the actual professional requirements and emotional demands of good mentorship. Whatever the cause, under these conditions, mentorships are likely to be marginalized.

What guidelines should mentors follow in selecting protégés? Research indicates that mentors in most fields generally select protégés with obvious talent and career potential. Juniors, who earn the label "fast-tracker" based on their past achievements and the perception that they will be successful, usually are appealing to mentors. These protégés favorably reflect the mentor's competence in developing talent and they eventually may become valued colleagues to the mentor. Communication skills, emotional stability, ambition, initiative, intelligence, and loyalty are other important traits. In addition, mentors should seek protégés who share their interests and have similar career aspirations.

In business settings, mentorships that begin informally often are more effective than those that are brokered or "arranged." The mutual understanding, respect, and trust that naturally evolve in an informally developed mentorship increase the chances that both parties will find the experience satisfying. We should always remember that mentorships, first and foremost, are relationships. As in a marriage, the freedom to choose for both the mentor and protégé provides grounding for mutual commitment and satisfaction. In general, mentors should be cautious and intentional in selecting their protégés.

Key Components

- *Decide in advance the maximum number of protégés you can mentor and maintain excellence.*

- *Identify the personal qualities, interests, and aspirations of protégés that make them a good "match" before committing to a mentorship.*
- *Commit to mentor only after some period of informal work and interaction with a prospective protégé.*
- *Remain vigilant to symptoms of mentor burnout.*
- *Honestly consider your motivation for mentoring.*

2
Know Your Protégés

Mary, a senior partner in a multinational law firm, noticed the exceptional work and unusual talent of Brian, a junior lawyer in her division. Mary then decided to mentor Brian. In the early phase of the mentorship, she watched Brian in various contexts and went out of her way to talk to him about his short-term plans, personal interests, and his career aspirations. She made arrangements to work with Brian on cases and gave him a variety of assignments in order for him to get a well-rounded applied education as a lawyer. Mary discerned Brian's strengths in the area of litigation and assigned him cases in this specialty. She also became proficient at "reading" Brian's nonverbal behavior, particularly his signals of distress. She responded to these indicators with inquiry and wise counsel—helping Brian to take stock of himself before working his way into a self-destructive frenzy.

Outstanding mentors study their protégés—learning about each one of them from the inside out. They actually become students of their protégés, attempting to master each one as they would attempt to master chemistry, history, or math. They discern the protégé's distinct mix of talents and vulnerabilities. Mentors observe protégés in various situations, listen to them, and show interest in their dreams and aspirations. They are especially attentive to the protégé's fears and personal challenges—acknowledging them as real but refusing to let the protégé see them as insurmountable.

What is the most important outcome of the deliberate study of a protégé? We propose that it is the ability to name the protégé's prominent gifts—naming them accurately, thoroughly, and always specific to the individual. Although each person you mentor will have a unique blend of talents, and perhaps one or more area of notable capability, many protégés are not as certain about their gifts as you initially might think. Protégés often err in either overestimating or underestimating their abilities. Sometimes their self-appraisals are flat out off track.

In naming the protégé's gifts and talents—making explicit what is often implicit—a powerful but necessary shift occurs in the protégé's conception of him or herself. The shift sets the course for a more promising career. But the neophyte requires the seasoned mentor's validation before the course is set into motion. Once protégés see themselves for who they really are, they are then in a position to build on their strengths and overcome their weaknesses. These are the results of seeing themselves through the sharp lens of their mentor.

To obtain an insightful understanding of protégés, mentors need to have a personal relationship with them. And the type of understanding of which we speak is more than knowing a protégé's name, rank, and serial number. It is a knowledge garnered through substantial observation, frequent interaction, and intense involvement—a real relationship. Research shows that the frequency and quality of face-to-face interaction predict mentorship success. This means that excellent mentors are accessible and available. But they also need to exhibit the human skills of listening, caring, communicating openly, and giving constructive feedback. To conclude, taking the time to truly know protégés is arguably the most important of the mentoring virtues.

Key Components

- *Deliberately study and learn about your protégés.*
- *Identify and label protégés' talents and strengths and then communicate these insights to them.*
- *Acknowledge protégé fears and comparative weaknesses without allowing them to distract or overwhelm.*
- *Look for patterns in protégés that occur across various settings, relationships, and type of assignment.*
- *Above all, spend time with protégés and understand mentoring as a relationship.*

3
Expect Excellence (and Nothing Less)

As a second-year Ph.D. student in a large psychology graduate program, Cliff began doing research under the supervision of Dr. Wright, an eminent scholar in Cliff's area of interest. From the outset, Dr. Wright was supportive and encouraging but simultaneously challenging. He made it clear to Cliff early on that he would only support Cliff to present and publish work that was exceptionally well-conceived and painstakingly polished. When Cliff's work fell short of that expectation, Dr. Wright pulled him aside and said, "Cliff, I'm not here to do mediocre work and neither are you. This work is not indicative of the scholar I know you to be. Try it again." Although sometimes he was annoyed or disheartened by his mentor's stringent requirements, Cliff was about to establish an impressive track record of publications in his field. Upon earning his doctorate and beginning his career as a newly minted psychologist, he was surprised to discover how much he had internalized his mentor's work ethic. Cliff himself became known as an exacting and careful researcher, and this reputation paid off in the form of marked success in grant funding and scholarly publication.

No one starts out as a gold medalist, not even an exceptional athlete who has an abundance of natural talent. An athlete develops into a superstar through hard work and practice, and this is true of top performers in every field. But excellence also must be expected. How do mentors set expectations of excellence? And, how does a mentor help protégés differentiate excellence from perfection? There are several crucial steps in generating excellence without disheartening or overwhelming protégés.

First, mentors never settle for mediocrity. People tend to perform at the level of their own internalized standards. Often they settle for less. Settling for mediocrity undermines performance because it lowers expectations. Paradoxically, most people are more capable than they think. They need a change in expectations. Here is an important rule: Mentors should expect more of their protégés than their protégés typically expect of themselves. This raises their expectations and lifts their performance.

Second, mentors communicate expectations for excellence. Research on parenting, supervising, and mentoring consistently shows that juniors rise to meet the expectations of mentors—particularly when the mentorship is characterized by trust, support, and mutual respect. Mentors provide a strong sense of inspirational motivation. They communicate high performance expectations through two salient channels. They first model confidence, competence, professionalism, and strong adherence to standards of excellence. They understand the importance of asking of others only what they first ask of themselves. By demanding excellence of themselves, they indirectly but resoundingly voice their high expectations of their protégés.

Then they directly verbalize their high expectations to protégés. They simultaneously communicate unwavering confidence in the protégé's capacity for meeting and even exceeding expectations. Even the most gifted protégé, at times, may lack confidence in some areas, performing only to the level of their modest expectations. This all can change when the mentor provides a vision of the protégé as talented, competent, and capable of high-level achievement.

What makes mentors ineffective in exacting expectations? Mentors can fail their protégés in three notable ways—all of which can be costly. These mistakes undermine the ability of protégés to realize their potential, and neither the protégé nor mentor reaps maximal returns. First, mentors may set their expectations too low. Low expectations fail to challenge protégés to be the best they can be. Although mentors may be kind, caring, and have good intentions, the net effect of their modest requirements is pervasive mediocrity. Only the most self-directed and motivated protégés will thrive when expectations are low.

Second, mentors may make stringent demands for excellence without simultaneously instilling confidence in protégés' capacity to meet these challenges. Without equipment and provisions, protégés are expected to make the journey from neophyte to excellent performer. For the protégé, this is disheartening and undermining. Third, mentors may—intentionally or not—send expectations for perfection. Unattainable and destructive, demands for flawless performance sabotage the efforts of the most well-intended mentor. Unable to reach perfection, protégés can become disenchanted, hopeless, and depressed. Ironically, many excellent protégés are already dangerously perfectionistic. The excellent mentor will detect and refute perfectionism while encouraging excellence and praising approximations to this goal.

Key Components

- *Set high expectations and communicate them clearly.*
- *Model the same excellence you expect from protégés.*
- *Demonstrate confidence in the protégé's capacity to meet your expectations.*
- *Never endorse perfection as a legitimate goal.*

4
Affirm, Affirm, Affirm, and Then Affirm Some More

When Hannah first met Beth at a regional denomination meeting for pastors, she saw a bright, articulate, but somewhat insecure new pastor. Beth had recently joined a nearby church as the associate pastor and was already struggling with congregational expectations and her own fears about being an "imposter." She perceived herself as ill-suited for the pastoral role. As an accomplished senior pastor, and the only other female pastor in the district, Hannah immediately knew she wanted to mentor Beth. Although she offered Beth numerous practical tips on preaching and inundated her with helpful resources, Hannah soon realized what Beth needed the most—affirmation. One afternoon, looking across her desk at Beth, Hannah said in a firm but caring voice "Beth, I know you're struggling right now, but hear this: You belong in the pastorate. I've seen you preach, and I know your heart. I believe God meant you to be a pastor. I'm glad you're here." Beth immediately began to sob and then described her parents' disapproval of her career choice and calling to the ministry. During the next several months, Hannah offered strong and unrelenting affirmation. Beth responded with increasing confidence and improved performance. As time went on, Beth's need for consistent affirmation decreased, and Hannah was able to turn to more career-oriented issues in mentoring.

People need to feel good about themselves and affirmation is the key to a feeling of well-being. Therefore, the need to be affirmed is human. As Dr.

Martin Luther King, Jr., once said, "The only time people do not like praise is when too much of it is going toward someone else." In mentorship, where the stakes are high and the pressure to succeed is intense, there can be no shortage of affirmation. If you could do only one thing as a mentor, affirm your protégés.

You can affirm protégés in two ways. You can affirm them as people. This is the most important type of affirmation. This is an acknowledgement of a person's inherent worth. Affirming protégés as people should be unconditional and independent of their performance. You can also affirm protégés as professionals. This is an acknowledgment of their achievements. Although affirming protégés as professionals should be conditional and dependent on their performance, be careful to affirm them as they make progress in the pursuit of excellence. Withholding affirmation until goals are achieved is usually a mistake.

Seize every opportunity to give affirmation. But never send the wrong message that a protégé's worth is contingent on performance. The bottom line is this: Affirmation is an artful blending of personal acceptance and professional endorsement. When mentors affirm their protégés, they communicate an unequivocal belief in the protégé. When protégés doubt themselves, mentors show confidence in them. When protégés take reasonable risks, mentors give their approval, and when protégés err, mentors remain serene.

Many protégés fear that they are "imposters," that if they were really known, they would not be accepted. Living in perpetual trepidation that their inadequacies will be discovered, these junior professionals remain inhibited and stunted in their development until affirmed by a mentor. The unflagging faith and confidence of a mentor may have a nearly miraculous effect on a protégé's self-confidence. Excellent mentors provide an affirmation-rich environment where protégés can experiment with their new identities and ride the tumultuous waves that accompany change and growth.

There are two primary components of affirmation. First, affirming mentors communicate and demonstrate faith in the protégé's ability and trust in the protégé's judgment. Research indicates that when protégés feel accepted and confirmed by a mentor, they are more willing to trust the mentor, believe in themselves, and accept increasingly challenging tasks. Affirmed protégés exude confidence. They are assured of acceptance—even when they fail.

The second component is more subtle and demanding of the mentor. Excellent mentors are so tuned into their protégés that they can discern the protégés' unique potential. The discernment may cover career and personal potential. We call this blessing. Psychologist Daniel Levinson believes that each protégé harbors a personal "dream" for adult life—a vision of what the person might achieve and become. A mentor works to discern and then nourish this dream. The mentor helps the protégé articulate the dream, and then blesses the protégé by affirming that the dream is possible. In so doing, the mentor sets the protégé into creative flight—offering the confidence and affirmation the protégé requires to get started. Of course, mentors must simultaneously temper unrealistic dreams, bringing the wisdom of experience to bear on the protégé's aspirations. Nonetheless, affirming is something every mentor can do.

Key Components

- *Always and unconditionally affirm your protégé as a person of great value.*
- *Regularly affirm your protégé's professional performance.*
- *Instill confidence in your protégés to help them overcome self-doubt and the "imposter syndrome."*
- *Seek to discern and then endorse your protégé's life and career "dream." Then, work diligently to help him or her achieve it.*
- *Gently shed light on unrealistic aspirations and find ways to affirm protégés even in the face of short-term failure.*

5
Provide Sponsorship

As the principal of a large suburban high school, Burt took notice of Jennifer, one of his brightest and most creative young teachers. Not only was Jennifer a gifted teacher and immensely popular with students and colleagues, she also was ambitious and curious about opportunities in educational leadership. Sensing that

Jennifer would benefit from some career assistance, Burt urged her to apply for the district's competitive M.A. tuition-remission program. He wrote her a stellar letter of recommendation and within two years, Jennifer had completed her master's degree. Burt then recommended her to the superintendent for the very competitive administrative training program (a pipeline for future principals). Along the way, Burt invited Jennifer to some important district meetings where he introduced her to key leadership personnel and got her assigned to some high profile committees and projects. Within five years, Jennifer took over the principal position at a large high school. Several years later, she became the assistant superintendent of a large neighboring school district.

No one can seize an opportunity if the door is shut. Sometimes mentors can open doors that protégés cannot open for themselves. They can endorse protégés' membership in important organizations, invite them to exclusive meetings, and endorse them for work on special or high-visibility projects. Mentors may introduce protégés to important individuals in the organization or in their profession. Mentors can help promising protégés to make presentations at conferences or participate in important meetings. Studies of distinguished (Nobel prize-winning) scientists show that sponsorship is often a critical component of gaining eminence in one's career. Successful scientists often study under leading researchers and, in turn, themselves sponsor juniors.

Sponsorship carries with it a sharing of power. As the protégé is associated with the mentor, and the mentor endorses the protégé's work, others accord the protégé *reflective power*—power of the mentor by extension. Reflective power can melt barriers, open doors, and provide access to influential people who normally would not be accessible to a protégé. The mentor's reflective power can be thought of as a sort of protégé shield. This shield, bearing the mentor's coat of arms, communicates to others in the field that the protégé has the backing, support, and promotion of a person of prominence.

Like the other skill-based elements of mentoring, effective sponsorship requires thoughtful intention. Accurate sponsorship demands familiarity with a protégé's specific career aspirations. Mentors must tailor sponsorship efforts to the protégé's unique life dream. Familiarity with a protégé's personal dream should help the mentor select organizations, meetings, committees, and other uniquely targeted opportunities for the protégé. You might consider this "precision sponsorship."

Sponsorship allows a fledgling professional to try new behaviors and hone the skills needed for success in any organization. This is critical for early career success, and it could make the difference in how far someone advances professionally. Certainly, with sponsorship come risks. Poor performance by a sponsored protégé could negatively impact the mentor's stature and ultimately, the ability to provide sponsorship in the future.

Key Components

- *Discern your protégé's unique career dream.*
- *Consider which opportunities (e.g., committees, organizations, projects, professional experiences) would best prepare the protégé to achieve this dream.*
- *Use your status and influence to help the protégé gain entry to groups and experiences that could be career enhancing.*
- *Allow the protégé to serve as your emissary at times—shielded by your reflective power and functioning on your behalf.*

6
Be a Teacher and a Coach

Although he was only four years Jim's senior in the company and only a couple of years older, Noel quickly became one of Jim's most important career mentors. The mentorship formed when Jim became a management-trainee. A relatively junior manager himself, Noel had established himself as a productive and well-liked member of the company. He quickly saw Jim as bright and promising and took him under his tutelage. He advised Jim about how he should present himself, who he should get to know, and whom he should avoid. He guided Jim on several difficult projects—pointing out the critical components and carefully teaching him the process. Noel helped him to prepare for important meetings and presentations, cautioning him regarding common mistakes. When Jim succeeded, Noel celebrated. When Jim fell short of expectations, Noel helped him to learn from the experience and move on.

If you teach, protégés will learn. Take time to give direct and explicit instruction. Excellent mentors provide knowledge, make recommendations, offer consultation, and stimulate motivation with encouragement. Their broad perspectives and experiences in the field make them attractive to potential protégés.

It is not surprising that the obituaries of highly regarded educators often highlight their profound gifts as mentors. They have often guided generations of student protégés. Nor is it surprising that great mentors frequently are described as patient and effective teachers. No matter the field of study, the nature of the discipline, or the characteristics of the protégé, good mentoring requires good teaching. We began this book with the words of Sophocles: "the reasonable thing is to learn from those who can teach." Quite frankly, if you have nothing to teach, or if you are unable to teach what you know, then do not presume to mentor. Protégés are drawn to those who teach: individuals who deliberately instruct and demonstrate the salient behaviors of a seasoned master in the protégé's field of interest.

Teaching often takes the form of direct training and information sharing. Mentors bolster a protégé's technical competence by providing knowledge and refining specific professional skills. Excellent mentors are eager and invested teachers. In contrast to the reluctant guru who occasionally rewards the dogged seeker with small nuggets of wisdom, the outstanding mentor creates opportunities to give advice, recount relevant experiences, and provide consultation on challenges that lie ahead. Good mentors are inherently educators. They understand that learning is a catalyst to growth.

Although most teaching is formal, protégé's also benefit from vicarious instruction that occurs through mentor storytelling. Some mentors are particularly effective at informally transferring knowledge about the workplace. They describe case examples of predecessors who have succeeded and failed. Some mentors use metaphors while others prefer to impart personal wisdom born out of their experience. They tell stories of their own successes and failures to shape and prepare protégés. Of course, it is essential that mentors only self-disclose for the purpose of teaching. Self-disclosure in the service of self-adulation or selfish catharsis is nearly always counter-productive. But keep this principle in mind: Self-disclosure is an adjunct to, not a substitute for, overt and direct forms of teaching.

Mentors provide protégés with crucial insider information, but they avoid gossip. Through their teaching, they cover a range of topics. They instruct protégés about the subtleties of local politics and organizational power. Good mentors teach protégés strategies for managing conflict, and coach them on setting short- and long-term goals. Also, they teach protégés the norms that set the acceptable range of behaviors.

Finally, good mentors understand when it is helpful to use a particular instructional strategy. Although the sharing of direct advice and instruction may be particularly important early in the mentorship, protégés may require less direct information-giving and teaching as the relationship matures. As protégés become increasingly confident and competent, they may operate with more independence. Therefore, teaching should be most active early in the mentoring process.

Key Components

- *Give direct and explicit instruction on the various roles and functions required in your vocation.*
- *Intentionally demonstrate and describe complex professional skills.*
- *Seize opportunities for training and instruction through story-telling and using metaphors.*
- *Help protégés understand and respect organizational politics and implicit group norms while avoiding gossip.*
- *Gradually decrease the amount of direct teaching as protégés develop and succeed.*

7
Encourage and Support

When Nancy landed a slot in an extremely competitive university doctoral program, she wondered if she had somehow slipped in by mistake. A divorced mother of three and a mid-career student, she wondered if she really "belonged" in graduate school. Although her mentor, Dr. Abrams, had selected Nancy largely due to her extremely high test scores and skillful writing ability, Nancy continued to doubt her own potential. During the first two years of the mentorship, Dr. Abrams recognized Nancy's self-doubt and therefore gave her strong and consistent encouragement and support. Not only did Dr. Abrams intently listen to Nancy's concerns about balancing the roles of mother and student, he often reminded her that she was selected into the program because she was exceptionally talented and someone he expected to be successful. So consistent was Dr. Abrams' encouragement and support, Nancy began to see herself through his positive and confident lens.

You may not master all the skills of mentoring, but chances are protégés will appreciate your efforts if you encourage them and provide them with emotional support. Famous psychologist, Carl Rogers, theorized that for growth to occur in counseling, a counselor needs to be kind, warm, and willing to offer unconditional positive regard to clients. Specific counseling techniques and therapeutic procedures were less important, in his opinion, than basic warmth and acceptance. Indeed, decades of research on helping relationships (counseling, psychotherapy, and mentoring) confirm his theory. People thrive when they feel safe, valued, and well supported. When a mentor is friendly, open, approachable, and consistently encouraging, protégés are more at ease with risk-taking, more assured that they can succeed, and more comfortable asking for advice and assistance.

Encouragement and support are always valuable. But there are times when they are especially necessary. Beginners in any field often experience the anxiety that accompanies facing new challenges. Other protégés encounter difficult times personally or professionally. Numerous studies, across a range of professions and mentoring contexts, find that encouragement and support are among the most important mentoring functions.

Here is a word of caution: Although encouragement and support may seem easy to give, they often are not. In fact, these skills may be difficult to learn. Like new counselors struggling to master the seemingly simple subtleties of genuine warmth and accurate listening, mentors may struggle with the fine art of encouragement and support. The greatest struggle may be with a protégé who is bright and self-confident. Mentors may as-

sume erroneously that these individuals do not need that type of encouragement. But their assumption may be dead wrong. Then there are mentors who are too busy to lend emotional support, while still others may be
uncomfortable in the encourager role. For whatever reason, failure to encourage and support diminishes the strength and value of the mentorship.

Encouragement and support are necessary throughout a mentoring relationship. They are especially crucial early in the mentorship when the
relationship between mentor and protégé is beginning to develop. But it
does not stop there. Mentors should seize every opportunity to speak a
kind word, lift a protégé's spirit, encourage a protégé to stay the course,
and be a sounding board when there is a need. The importance of encouragement and support cannot be overstated. Research consistently
shows that protégés appreciate mentors who display these qualities and
criticize those who do not.

Key Components

- *Expect even the most talented and confident protégé to benefit from en-
  couragement and support.*
- *Understand that while foundational to mentoring, encouragement and
  support are not easy to practice.*
- *Seek opportunities to offer support, praise, and encouragement.*
- *Supportive mentors are genuine, consistent, warm, and accepting.*

8
Offer Counsel in Difficult Times

*As a vice president in a nonprofit educational consulting organization, Dan
was in a position to mentor a number of junior professionals. Derek was one of
Dan's primary protégés. He benefited enormously from Dan's steady career advice, guidance, and support. In the second year of the mentorship, Derek went
through a painful divorce. He turned to Dan with questions about his own
competence, the organization's view of his personal problems, and even questions about whether his devotion to work had sabotaged his marriage. Although
Dan did not try to play the role of a professional counselor, he did advise Derek*

to worry less about the job, place a priority on his self-care, and avoid making significant career decisions in his current state of mind. He assured Derek that what others in the organization thought about his personal life would not be allowed to hamper his job security as long as he continued his excellent track record. Throughout the hardest phase of Derek's divorce, Dan counseled patience, self-care, and perspective-taking.

Mentoring is not professional counseling or therapy. But sooner or later, a protégé will ask for a mentor's counsel. Mentorships often occur during a phase of the protégé's life characterized by stress, change, and growing pains. Therefore, it is not surprising that mentorships occasionally include a dimension best described as *informal counseling*. Protégés benefit from discussing their problems with their mentor and exploring solutions. Most protégé concerns and difficulties can be clustered into three broad domains—developing professional competence and career satisfaction, managing professional relationships, and managing the competing demands of one's career and personal life.

Concerns bearing on competence and career satisfaction typically take the form of either perceived inadequacy—the *imposter syndrome*, or doubt about the extent of a match between protégé and career track. Buffeted by overwhelming demands, insecurity, or unsavory glimpses at the real life of the professional, the emotional needs of protégés may rise to the surface. They may want reassurance that they can succeed. They may want advice in how to navigate their career trajectories. In some cases, they may want permission to reconsider their career choice and to do so without the threat of reprisal or ridicule.

Concerns bearing on professional relationships take many forms. They may involve the management of difficult colleagues or supervisors. Take a protégé who seeks advice about handling a supervisor's unreasonable demands, hostility, an unfair evaluation, or inappropriate sexual overtures. In these types of situations, the mentor has to exercise great wisdom. When counseling in these situations, the mentor must be discrete and supportive—helping without parenting and protecting without smothering the protégé. At times, good counsel will require direct confrontation. Even excellent protégés commit snafus or exacerbate relational problems with colleagues.

Concerns regarding the management of career and other facets of protégés' personal lives are plentiful. Juggling roles is a common theme. Protégés may play a variety of roles such as junior professional, spouse, parent, child, and member of a community. In these various roles, they struggle with the stress of balancing their responsibilities and fragmented identities. They need guidance in how to be successful in each of their roles without compromising themselves in any one role.

How do mentors offer counsel? First, they should recognize their limitations and never pretend to be professional counselors. For example, mentors should not expect themselves to be able to help protégés with all of their problems, nor should they attempt to treat obvious mental health problems. Clearly, problems like severe depression or substance abuse disorders are out of the league of most mentors. When they encounter serious problems such as these, they should encourage the protégé to get professional counseling. Of course, when mentors themselves are mental health professionals, they must be ethical. They should maintain their boundaries, avoid a dual relationship, and refer the protégé to another professional.

Second, although they are not counseling professionals, mentors allow protégés to explore both personal and professional issues in the context of the mentorship. Skills such as active listening, accurate understanding of another's feelings, clarification of decision-making strategies, and assistance in goal setting help protégés to accept and overcome inner doubts and personal obstacles. Moreover, effective mentors listen, convey acceptance, normalize the existence of problems and distress, and facilitate problem solving. Protégés are profoundly helped by the mere willingness of the mentor to listen to and validate their concerns.

Third, mentors should not avoid the responsibility of offering wise counsel. They understand that offering counsel is inevitable in mentoring, that it may enhance the mentoring relationship, and that wise counsel can facilitate a protégé's personal and professional development.

Finally, mentors should discourage protégés from trying to use the mentorship for professional counseling or psychotherapy. Using a mentorship in this way can damage the relationship and end up producing a counterproductive experience. Therefore, mentors need discretion to know where their support begins and where their support ends. They also need to help protégés develop the discretion to know how to maintain their boundaries.

Key Components

- *Be open to discussing and exploring protégé concerns and difficulties.*
- *Actively listen, reflect feelings, and clarify alternatives.*
- *Offer unconditional acceptance and validate the protégé's experience.*
- *Accept your limitations; refer protégés to a professional when serious emotional disturbance emerges.*

9
Protect When Necessary

As a first-year resident in a competitive neurology residency program, Dr. Emily Myers came under the tutelage of Dr. Maria Chavez, her primary rotation supervisor and a senior member of the medical staff. Although Emily was an outstanding physician, she was somewhat eccentric and socially inept. Unbeknownst to Emily, she was often the brunt of behind-the-back teasing from other residents. Nonetheless, Dr. Chavez saw Emily as a talented young physician. She noticed that Emily's social eccentricities seemed to be lessening as her confidence and competence increased. During a faculty meeting to evaluate residents, several junior male members of the faculty began mimicking Emily's odd dress and habits. Dr. Chavez recognized this sabotaging behavior as the kind of thing that could easily undermine a resident's status in the program. She calmly but sternly stated, "the last time I checked gentlemen, fashionable dress and social grace were not evaluation criterion in our residency. Dr. Myers is one of my most promising residents. I hope that in the future you will limit your comments and observations to relevant concerns." That statement sent a clear message to the training faculty. Emily enjoyed the support and protection of her mentor. Although Emily became a successful graduate of the residency, she was never aware of her mentor's protective intervention.

The road to success can be lined with perils and danger. Some are obvious. Others are less so. Sometimes even the most talented protégé can be blindsided. Because mentors have traveled the road to success, they are more familiar with the signs of danger and should be prepared to protect their protégés. On occasion, the mentor must don armor, shield, and sword to discourage or repel an inappropriate attack.

Career threats take on many forms—bureaucratic entanglements, conflict with colleagues, hostile criticism, assignment to tasks likely to sabotage success, and one's own poor decision-making. A mentor who fails to respond expeditiously to such threats renders the protégé vulnerable to a range of negative outcomes—including career failure. When a protégé is threatened, mentor protection becomes crucial. Protection may take many forms such as publicly advocating for the protégé, directly confronting hostile parties (or their supervisors), creating short-cuts through bureaucratic red tape, and preventing the assignment of the protégé to low-visibility roles, or roles that are likely to overwhelm the protégé.

Effective protection demands calm and measured assertiveness. The credible mentor is deliberate but thoughtful in coming to the rescue of the protégé. Signs of outrage, indignation, and personal disturbance diminish the mentor's credibility. These signs telegraph either excess ego-involvement in the life of the protégé, or an arrogant view that no one should "dare" challenge or mistreat the mentor's affiliates. In either case, the mentor loses and his or her ability to protect decreases.

Protection, however, can be a double-edged sword. Mentors must carefully guard against overprotection, bullying, and turning a blind eye to real problems in protégé performance. An overprotective mentor often fails to recognize protégés' weaknesses and performance failures. This type of mentor will lose both power and credibility within an organization. Rather than being an admired advocate, he or she will be seen as an unreasonable avenger. Therefore, while it is essential to protect protégés, it is equally important to give honest feedback and confront protégés when necessary. Just as failure to protect a protégé may damage his or her professional identity and career, excessive or misinformed efforts at protection may undermine protégé autonomy and sabotage the mentor's credibility.

Key Components

- *Accept the fact that protégés will occasionally suffer career-inhibiting personal or political attacks.*

- *Respond expeditiously but calmly to unfair threats or attacks against a protégé; avoid the appearance of rage or indignation.*
- *Use protection sparingly; frequent intervention reduces mentor credibility.*
- *Honestly consider protégé contributions to professional conflicts.*
- *Never bully.*

10
Stimulate Growth
with Challenging Assignments

When Charlie assumed duties as the new assistant vice president for human resources, he developed a profound respect for Doug. Doug was his immediate boss and the vice president of the human resources division. Doug also was a remarkably accomplished speaker and motivator; he was well known in the company and in the larger training community for his leadership development workshops. Charlie was in awe of Doug. Doug immediately began to mentor Charlie. He provided direct teaching and coaching in the art of training, praised Charlie's early efforts, and pushed him to take an increasing role in the weekly workshops. Although initially terrified of being the "upfront" man, Charlie found that he not only survived each new challenge, but that he actually enjoyed himself. Several months later, with Charlie feeling reasonably confident in the presenter role, Doug announced to Charlie that it was time for Charlie to start "taking the reins." Doug had scheduled Charlie as the main speaker for an important executive leadership workshop in another city. Although Charlie was initially terrified, Doug reassured him that he was ready and noted, "I told them they were getting one of our best trainers." Charlie was well-received and his confidence was bolstered.

Change typically comes about through a deliberate process. Normally it does not take place overnight. Nor does it occur with one try. Protégé growth and development, for instance, are catalyzed when mentors create progressively more challenging assignments. Protégé competence and confidence typically increase at the same rate at which the mentor provides challenges. The assignment of challenging work is essential for both technical skill development and professional identity enhancement. Maximally useful assignments must be accompanied by both critical feedback and reinforcing praise.

Skillful mentors tailor assignments to the needs of protégés. They attempt to facilitate growth and development without overwhelming the protégé or inducing unwarranted failure. Here are three relevant guidelines.

First, shape performance through successive approximations. To shape means to improve gradually, to move someone closer to the expected performance. Incrementally more difficult assignments result in growth as long as the immediate expectations do not supercede the protégé's current level of ability. Therefore, find the optimal beginning point for each protégé and then shape according to the protégé's pace of development. Aim high. But do not start too high or too low. Furthermore, do not shape too fast or too slow. Above all, always find the right balance for each protégé.

Second, find the right challenge for your protégé. Regardless of your profession or work setting, each protégé is an individual. Each will present a unique blend of talents, interests, and personal qualities. Find progressively demanding jobs that match each protégé. For instance, two protégés may have similar backgrounds and experience; one may be introverted and socially phobic (though precise in written communication) while the other is outgoing and comedic (though prone to neglect attention to detail). These protégés require different challenges for maximal growth. While honoring each protégé's gifts, the challenging mentor with give assignments that are individually stretching.

Third, help protégés manage their anxiety. Performance anxiety comes with the territory of growth and development. Depending on how it is managed, anxiety can hinder or enhance the developing protégé. Here are steps for mentors to take. Teach protégés that anxiety is normal and that this is what they should anticipate. Encourage protégés to use anxiety as a source of motivation. Assist protégés in understanding that moderate anxiety can help them clear new hurdles of performance. And help protégés to recognize that the absence of anxiety can compromise good motivation.

Key Components

- *Deliberately challenge protégés with demanding assignments tailored to their abilities and performance thresholds.*

- *Shape performance through successive approximations to the desired goal.*
- *Avoid making demands that exceed protégé performance capacities.*
- *Help protégés accept, tolerate, and effectively manage anxiety in the face of new challenges.*

11
Give Protégés Exposure and Promote Their Visibility

Fresh out of college, Stuart began writing ad copy for some of the smallest accounts in a large Los Angeles advertisement firm. On several occasions, Marsha, the firm's creative director, came to Stuart with last minute "emergency" jobs. In each instance, Stuart worked long hours, did excellent work, and even helped Marsha fine tune the client presentation. Very impressed with Stuart's ability and work ethic, Marsha began grooming him for a larger role in the firm. Specifically, she began shunting some high profile client projects Stuart's way, paired him with one of the more successful artists in the firm, and began mentioning Stuart's successes to the other directors and partners. While careful not to overwhelm him, Marsha selected clients and projects that were especially well matched with Stuart's interests and strengths—helping ensure further success. Marsha made sure that clients would take note of Stuart's accomplishments, and many of them began to insist that Stuart direct their accounts. As Stuart's successes mounted, Marsha mentioned him frequently as a potential future director in the firm.

Trumpet your protégés' successes and expose them to the senior leaders in the organization. Organizational research shows that a salient component of early career socialization is the opportunity for junior professionals to demonstrate competence to others. As mentors expose protégés to new responsibilities and create individually tailored challenges, they must simultaneously seek out or create opportunities for public exposure. Outstanding mentors draw attention to their protégés by highlighting their contributions and achievements both laterally (to peers and colleagues) and vertically (to superiors). Of course, mentors must have their egos in check and feel secure within themselves. Otherwise, they will be threatened by the accolades and praise not coming their way.

The best way to generate visibility for protégés is to give them high-profile assignments. Working on important accounts, participating on influential committees, or landing a project that requires considerable interface with influential stakeholders are all excellent methods of enhancing positive exposure. Certainly, mentors must make sure protégés are prepared to meet the challenge. Otherwise, failure in high-visibility assignments can shake a protégé's confidence or ruin a mentor's credibility. Failure may also derail a protégé's rise in an organization. Protégés need the good judgment of the mentor to assure them that they are ready for the challenge and they also need to trust that the mentor's judgment is sound.

We recommend creating initial exposure and visibility via collaborative efforts with protégés. In the world of academe, mentors can co-author articles, team-teach, and co-present conference papers with graduate students or junior faculty. In business organizations, mentors can create sub-projects and collateral tasks suited to the person's talent and experience. Such collaborative efforts offer the protégé fame-by-association without incurring substantial risk. As protégé successes accrue, the mentor makes these successes public and searches for other opportunities for the protégé to build on the successes.

Key Components

- *Draw attention to protégés by highlighting their achievements to both your colleagues and superiors.*
- *Create opportunities for protégé collaboration on high-visibility projects.*
- *Promote positive protégé interface with influential stakeholders.*
- *Ensure that protégé successes and achievements are made visible within the organization.*

12
Nurture Creativity

Nearing retirement, Dr. Smith was delighted when Javier, a newly minted doctorate, accepted an assistant professorship at his college. As chair of the college's small psychology department, Dr. Smith had watched enrollment in

psychology courses steadily decline during the last decade. Things changed dra-
matically during Javier's first year on the job when students began excitedly
mentioning the "strange" new professor's classroom antics. Rather than lecture
constantly as was the custom in the department, Javier repeatedly arranged
for unconventional events to occur in his social psychology class; he appeared
in the dress and character of famous psychologists in his history of psychology
class and had students act the part of disordered clients in his abnormal psy-
chology class. In the classroom, Javier was energetic, challenging, unpre-
dictable, and given to imaginative role-plays and in-class demonstrations.
Although enrollment in psychology courses and interest in the psychology
major swelled, some professors in the department were put off by Javier's un-
conventional approach. Nonetheless, Dr. Smith praised Javier's creativity,
trumpeted his teaching excellence to the college dean, and encouraged Javier to
write about his teaching ideas. Not only did Javier advance rapidly, he be-
came a nationally known author on the topic of innovative teaching tech-
niques. He eventually became dean of instruction at a major university.

Everyone has something special and unique to offer. For some people, the uniqueness is more obvious than for others. Nevertheless, mentors should attempt to awaken the creativity and innovation that each protégé possesses. They should nurture their protégés' dreams and help them realize their special potentialities. Extensive research programs with children suggest that having a mentor correlates significantly with various measures of adult creative achievement. Sponsors or patrons nourish independence and creativity while intervening in the social system to prevent the hampering of protégé creativity. In this mentoring context, originality is endorsed and this often persists as an aspect of the protégé's adult professional identity.

The role of a mentor in nurturing creativity is analogous to the actions of a midwife. A mentor offers a protective sanctuary in which creativity is first recognized and encouraged. As protégés take risks or generate new ideas and innovative strategies, mentors applaud these efforts. They listen sincerely to tentative proposals and ideas and they ardently resist opportunities to ridicule and reject. Nurturing creativity also requires the mentor to temper idealism and dreamful expansiveness with the wisdom of experience and the discipline of reality. This is a difficult dance for no one really knows another's ultimate potential. But outstanding mentors err on the side of being flexible and affirming especially when protégés are just getting started and their creative potential is still unknown.

Who is better suited than a mentor to nurture creativity? Mentors themselves are typically creative. They model creativity by pursuing unusual solutions to problems, questioning accepted standards in the field, and displaying energetic excitement in the face of challenge. They are first hand exemplars.

Key Components

- *Encourage innovative thought and creative problem solving in protégés.*
- *Provide a safe haven for creative protégés to develop and experiment with novel approaches.*
- *Reinforce creativity while tempering over-expansiveness with reality and pragmatics.*
- *Model innovation and creative excitement for protégés.*

13
Provide Correction—Even When Painful

Ingrid had mentored Dana as a manager for a year. Dana, in many respects, was competent, creative, and savvy. Well-liked by customers, peers, and managers, Dana had only a couple of discernable shortcomings. She tended to complete tasks at the last minute and her preparation for major presentations was spotty. When confronted, she would gloss over the feedback with charm and humor. As a result, Ingrid expressed some serious reservations to Dana about the long-term impact of this behavior on her career and future with the company. Following a particularly disorganized presentation, Ingrid confronted Dana more forcefully than ever: "Dana, your presentation today was poorly prepared and unprofessional. It fell far below the level of excellence I would expect from someone with your talent. Not only are you doing yourself a disservice, your substandard work is beginning to reflect unfavorably on me. In order to continue as your mentor, I need to see a dramatic turn around in your planning and preparation."

No one is perfect. That's why even the sharpest protégé can benefit from constructive criticism. Failing to offer correction when it is needed is a disservice to the protégé. This omission reflects the mentor's incompetence, disinterest, or avoidance of conflict. Good mentors address sub-par performance and lack of attention to detail; they offer critical but constructive appraisals and point to methods of correction. Although encouraging creativity and innovation, mentors must simultaneously shine the light of realism and feasibility on enthusiastic (but sometimes unrealistic) protégé plans.

Timing is everything when providing correction. Critical reflection and performance feedback are most palatable and useful to the protégé who has gone through the initial phase of mentorship; personal insecurity becomes less troubling and confidence begins to take form. The mentor is sensitive to the protégé's level of development, tempering criticism with an appreciation of the protégé's confidence and capacity for constructive response to correction. Early in the mentorship, effective correction should be preceded by a healthy dose of affirmation and encouragement. As a mentorship seasons and the protégé develops, confrontation may become more direct, less buffered, and the protégé will not feel as threatened.

In addition to performance-based correction, mentors must also be willing to address unethical or unprofessional protégé behavior. Protégés vary in their understanding of what is ethically acceptable or in their commitment to behave ethically. In an effort to achieve rapid success, the overzealous protégé may cut ethical corners such as by lying or taking credit for work done by others. In confronting a protégé's unethical behavior, mentors offer an essential service to the profession and to the protégé. The reputation of the profession is spared as are serious consequences for the protégé.

Mentors also should be attuned to the protégés' personal health. They can help protégés address unhealthy work habits (e.g., compulsive overworking, social isolation, pervasive conflict with coworkers) and evidence of personal distress (e.g., depression, anxiety, chronic anger). They can help protégés realize that problem work habits interfere with both long-term health and career success. Mentors should understand that dysfunctional work habits and personal distress can emanate from one of two primary sources. *State disturbances* are situational; the protégé is impacted or overwhelmed by circumstances, cumulative stress, or on-the-job events. State disturbances are transient; the prognosis for constructive change is good. *Trait disturbances*, on the other hand, are characterological; they are rooted in the very foundation of the protégé's personality. Although trait disturbances (e.g., compulsivity, pervasive self-doubt, volatile anger) must be confronted, they are more difficult to change than state disturbances. Mentors need a potent intervention that may require the assistance of a neutral health professional.

Finally, confrontation can be paradoxical. On the one hand, confronting a protégé may surface some pain, but it shows caring. On the other hand, avoiding a confrontation may spare the protégé some pain, but causes greater vulnerability to costly errors and unchecked dysfunction. Mentors who really care confront problem behavior.

Key Components

- *Confront self-defeating, unprofessional, or career-inhibiting protégé behavior.*
- *Temper confrontation with realistic affirmation—especially early on.*
- *Quickly address unethical, unprofessional, and illegal protégé behavior.*
- *Kindly confront personal distress and sabotaging work habits without assuming a mental health practitioner role.*
- *Recognize that appropriate confrontation builds trust.*

14
Narrate Growth and Development

With graduate degrees in both management and psychology, Wayne was happy as a lark to land his first job working for a large national consulting firm. The firm specialized in managerial selection and training. Wayne's supervisor, Ron, was an accomplished psychologist and head of training for the firm. Ron had a knack for developing talent. So it was natural for him to see Wayne as an asset to the organization. He also enjoyed interacting with Wayne, and he admired Wayne's ambition and interest in learning the ins and outs of consulting. As their mentorship developed, Ron watched Wayne nervously deliver his first training workshops and tentatively write his initial managerial selection reports. After each such initial foray into consulting work, Ron would take Wayne aside and comment on what he had done well and why this was an important step along the way to mastering consulting skills. As time moved on, Ron discontinued the practice of commenting on each and every report or workshop, but he continued to observe Wayne's performance and made a mental note of his increasing competence and confidence. From time to time, Ron would just smile and make supportive statements such as: "You've come a long way Wayne," or "You're getting very close to running the workshops on your own, how does that feel?" Long after the mentorship had ended, Wayne recalled that Ron's kind, consistent, and honest narration of his progress was a key ingredient in developing his professional self-confidence.

A protégé needs a mentor to provide commentary, to describe the protégé's movement and change. No one is better situated to narrate the protégé's professional growth and personal development than a mentor. Naïve and overwhelmed, the protégé can develop tunnel vision—seeing only the hurdles yet to be cleared while overlooking the milestones and progress in the rearview mirror. Seasoned and observant, the mentor can lend the "big-picture" view, helping the protégé to appreciate the distance covered as well as the terrain ahead.

Having his or her journey narrated, especially milestones achieved and skills acquired, allows a protégé an occasional opportunity to savor small gains and appreciate good work. To narrate effectively, mentors must be intentional, observant, and caring. Mentors see even modest gains in confidence and performance and describe these to the protégé. They note professional achievements and finds avenues for recognizing and even celebrating them. Mentors point out risks taken and label competency where they observe it. Mentors also help place minor setbacks and failures in perspective, detailing the larger picture of development and success. Putting these narrative skills together enables protégés to gain a realistic appreciation of how far they have come and an objective macro view of their professional progress.

A side benefit of a narrative approach is the strengthening of the mentoring bond. The mentor will probably be the only person in the protégé's life who takes time to accurately and affirmatively acknowledge growth and change. This mentoring function builds protégé esteem, enhances confidence, and strengthens the mentor–protégé alliance. Good narration demonstrates caring and commitment. Mentors who narrate well forever hold a special place in the lives of their protégés. They tell the real story of growth, change, and development—a story that will always be etched in the minds of protégés.

Key Components

- *Attend carefully to your protégé's small gains and important milestones.*
- *Narrate your observations of development and achievement.*
- *Use these gains to highlight how far your protégé has traveled on the professional journey.*
- *Understand that your affirmative narration will be quite meaningful to your protégé and that it will strengthen the mentorship bond.*

15
Self-Disclose When Appropriate

Jin was petrified when it came to public speaking. Although she was bright and confident in most areas, she had a long-standing public speaking phobia. Of course, this fear substantially hampered her performance in law school, and as she began a clerkship at a major law firm, she worried that Stephen, her supervising attorney and mentor would discover this shortcoming and then reject her. Although her legal research and written briefs were outstanding, she avoided Stephen's invitations to participate in depositions and oral briefings. Recognizing Jin's social reticence, Stephen disclosed his own struggle with public speaking earlier in his career. Smiling kindly he said: "Jin, you remind me of myself in law school. I had a profound fear of speaking and felt like I was going to shake to death every time I had to get up in front of class. I managed to work through it just by doing it more often, forcing myself to accept speaking engagements, and refusing to get too down on myself. I still get anxious before courtroom appearances, but I deal with it and people even say I come off pretty well!" Surprised to learn about Stephen's similar struggle, the revelation served as an impetus for Jin. She not only felt relief, she sought outside coaching and counseling to sharpen her speaking skills.

Authentic self-disclosure has the potential to create more poignant learning, more meaningful change, and a more enduring bond than any other mentor intervention. Sometimes mentors disclose important pieces of their own history such as critical turning points in their development. Sometimes they disclose their own fears, apprehensions, and struggles. Of course, they share their successes as well. But protégés can be deeply impacted when they hear the less glamorous side of the mentor's personal story. Self-disclosure can be a source of encouragement. Protégés can discover that success does not come without struggle and their mentor is a living example. Seasoned and self-aware mentors also are comfortable disclosing how the mentorship affects them and what they value most in the protégé. Such disclosure models self-awareness and a willingness to be authentic in the relationship.

Because self-disclosure can enhance intimacy and connection in a relationship, it is not surprising that protégés in many fields rate the willingness to self-disclose as one of the most important qualities in a mentor. When mentors share meaningful experiences or feelings, they show what it means to be authentic and they model self-exploration. In essence, the thoughtfully revealing mentor opens a window into the self and allows the protégé a glimpse inside. These forays into the life of the mentor must be selective, well timed, and tailored to the protégé's current needs and experiences. When a protégé suffers from self-doubt, the mentor might share early career anxieties. When a protégé strains to juggle work and family responsibilities, the mentor might relate personal strategies that proved helpful.

When self-disclosure is thoughtful, cautious, and geared to normalizing the protégé's experience, it can be life-changing. Self-disclosure communicates authenticity; it metacommunicates investment in and caring for the protégé. Moreover, it strengthens the bond between the mentor and protégé. But here is a word of caution. Mentors should remain vigilant to any sign that their self-disclosures are leading to codependency or romantic involvement.

Self-disclosure is finally an opportunity to demonstrate humility. Genuine and humble mentors disclose their own mistakes and weaknesses; they use their failings to provide vicarious learning experiences for their protégés. Such mentors shun adulation and work against misconceptions born of idealization. Exceptional mentors avoid offering themselves as *mastery* models (those who have conquered challenges and adversity and who no longer suffer from weakness, fear, or failing). Instead, they are models of *coping* (those who retain a good measure of imperfection yet manage to cope effectively through wisdom painfully acquired).

We use the phrase "when appropriate" for good reason. Self-disclosure can be used to great benefit or detriment. The difference is simply this: appropriate self-disclosure is done for the betterment of the protégé, while inappropriate self-disclosure is done for the gratification of the mentor. Self-gratifying self-disclosure is aimed at enhancing one's stature in the eyes of a protégé.

Key Components

- *Disclose salient personal experiences as a means of teaching, reassuring, and connecting with protégés.*
- *Model humility and self-exploration through appropriate self-disclosure.*
- *Offer protégés a model of coping, not a model of mastery.*
- *Appreciate the power of self-disclosure to heighten intimacy.*
- *Self-disclose only for the benefit of your protégé.*

16
Accept Increasing Friendship and Mutuality

Over a period of three years, Captain Sharp, the commanding officer of a Navy destroyer, had become particularly fond of his primary protégé, Lieutenant Gray. A smart, trustworthy, and ambitious young officer, Lieutenant Gray was also an excellent leader. In Captain Sharp's view, the lieutenant was just the sort of officer the Navy needed to retain and promote. During his tour as C.O., Captain Sharp had coached, encouraged, and counseled his protégé both to enhance his career and support his attempts to balance his roles as husband, father, and naval officer. During the final year of the active mentorship, the two had more frequent informal discussions about a military career, families, and life in general. Lieutenant Gray's family was often invited to dine with the Captain and his wife. By the time both officers moved to new commands, they were close friends. In the years that followed, the two stayed in close contact and Captain Sharp continued to offer guidance, support, and protection throughout the remainder of his career. Captain Sharp later described his protégé as "part junior officer, part son, and part friend."

As a protégé develops and a mentorship seasons, the excellent mentor welcomes and enjoys an increasingly mutual and collegial friendship. Mutuality is the shared respect, trust, and affection that evolve in a reciprocally beneficial mentoring relationship. Although benefits pertain primarily to the protégé during the early phases of the mentorship, later phases of mentorship may be marked by increasing reciprocity. As the protégé requires less direct teaching, training, and support, and as the protégé's confidence and independence increase, the mentorship may evolve into a relationship that takes on new dimensions. Research confirms that protégés find this mutual support an essential part of mentoring. The experience of giving and receiving in a safe mentorship prepares protégés to become colleagues to their mentors and to others.

Mutuality requires willingness to give and take on the part of the mentor. Mentors give of themselves in ways we have already described. They authentically self-disclose, demonstrate warmth and honesty, provide evidence of trust in the protégé by offering them participation in high-stake tasks, and they provide access to important personal and organizational information. Mutuality also requires receiving, a willingness to enjoy the protégé, and acknowledge enjoyment of the growing collegial bond. While honoring the personal boundaries needed to maintain a professional relationship, secure mentors allow themselves to see the protégé as a junior colleague. The mentor begins to enjoy the shared interests, emotional connection, and synergistic energy that blossom from investment in the mentorship.

Most protégés like the collegiality that emerges from a maturing mentorship. Not all protégés, however, find this transition comfortable. Some protégés hold personally rigid or culturally hierarchical views of seniors. For these protégés, collegiality with a supervisor is destabilizing and disorienting. Some protégés hold such deep idealization of their mentors that they could not imagine themselves having anything of substance to offer. In these cases, mentors have to be sensitive to the needs of the protégé. They simply cannot hold the same expectations of collegiality for every protégé nor expect mutuality to develop at the same pace in each mentorship.

Key Components

- *Accept and encourage gradually increasing friendship and collegiality with protégés.*
- *Recognize that protégés experience increasing mutuality as profession-ally validating.*
- *Communicate enjoyment of your increasing friendship with protégés.*
- *Respect protégé preferences for traditional hierarchical relationships; never force mutuality or familiarity.*

17
Teach Faceting

Kendra was in awe of Janice, her mentor of three years in a large university political science department. As a relatively new faculty member, Kendra worked incredibly long hours, and she occasionally became obsessed about get-ting grants and achieving tenure. At these times, Janice seemed to ask just the right questions about her life outside of the university. She would ask how Kendra's husband was, how often she was getting out to go running (some-thing Janice and Kendra both enjoyed), and about what novel Kendra was reading (her primary pastime outside of work). At times, Janice would actu-ally say something like, "this is just a job Kendra, don't pretend it's your whole life. Do good work then go home and take care of your marriage, your health, and your life in novels!" Perhaps most convincing, Janice modeled reasonable work hours, wide-ranging hobbies and interests, and a significant commit-ment to spending time with her family.

The single most time-tested and dependable mantra emanating from the lips of financial advisors the world over is this: diversify! Stocks surge and fall, bond markets sag, real estate follows regional economic whims. The best protection: spread your assets around. As the cliché warns, "don't put all your eggs in one basket." This advice applies to other areas of life as well. Strangely, far too few mentors offer similar advice to their protégés when it comes to charting a career course.

Various strands of health research indicate that people with a breadth of interests and time investments are better adjusted and more resilient in the face of adversity. When a person's life contains more than a single facet (e.g., work, economic achievement), he or she is said to be "multifaceted" and comparatively better off than the singularly focused peer. By developing a range of interests and skills, a person is faceting. It is essential to practice faceting in one's personal life and helpful to do the same in the world of work.

Excellent mentors understand that the protégé whose only outlet is work is ill-prepared for life and that the protégé who specializes only in one focused area of work is ill-prepared for a career. In the case of unanticipated job-loss or career-ending illness, the career-only protégé is emotionally destitute and confused. Having invested little in family, relationships external to work, or absorbing hobbies and recreational involvement, this person lacks the faceting to adjust and move ahead. Similarly, the protégé who rejects opportunities to develop new specialties or practice new approaches becomes occupationally marginalized and vulnerable when organizations change or seek innovation.

So how does the mentor help a protégé become faceted? There are two primary methods. First, ask about the breadth of a protégé's life interests and involvements. Demonstration of interest and concern in a protégé's activities, hobbies, and important relationships external to work communicates genuine interest in the whole person. Such benign inquiries telegraph a valuing of multifaceted lifestyles. Without violating privacy or becoming intrusive, the mentor shows genuine interest in the protégé as both a person and a junior professional. This mentor behavior says to the protégé: "all of your life commitments, involvements, and interests are important. Remember work is only one slice of who you are."

The second method for helping a protégé become faceted could be more difficult for some mentors. It requires modeling. When mentors are workaholics with few interests external to the job, they are ineffective models of faceting. As is true in parenting and teaching, subordinates learn by watching (and only secondarily by listening). The mentor's office may be adorned with pictures of family and the mentor may inquire about the protégé's own family, and yet work 90 hours a week. Alternatively, mentors can model spending time with loved ones, active involvement in hobbies, having close personal friendships, and willingness to experiment with new job tasks and even career opportunities. They should practice what they preach and live by the rule: "Do as I do, not simply as I say." The message they send should be clear: I am more than my current job title, and if my job ended tomorrow, only one facet of my life would change.

Key Components

- *Model a multifaceted lifestyle and refuse to make work your only life commitment.*
- *Inquire as to your protégé's family, leisure, and community connections and reinforce these important life involvements.*
- *Remind protégés that they are more than the sum of their job titles and do not reinforce exclusive devotion to work.*
- *Encourage protégés to frequently experiment with new specialties and innovations—increasing their career faceting and marketability.*

18
Be an Intentional Model

As a second-year clinical psychology doctoral student, Daniel was flattered when Dr. Mason, a forensic psychologist and senior faculty member, agreed to serve as Daniel's program advisor and mentor. Almost from the outset, Dr. Mason asked Daniel to accompany him to evaluation sessions, court appearances, and professional meetings in which he was an invited speaker. While his peers rarely had individual meetings with their mentors, Daniel was spending several hours each week watching Dr. Mason "do" forensic psychology. As time went on, Daniel was asked to take increasing responsibility for assisting with parts of the evaluations, co-teaching one of Dr. Mason's undergraduate courses, co-presenting papers at meetings, and even assisting with courtroom presentations. Through his frequent first-hand observation of Dr. Mason's work with clients, colleagues, students, and even lay audiences,

Daniel developed significant confidence as a junior professional himself. When he completed his doctoral program, Daniel was so comfortable in his role as a professional that colleagues often mistook him for a much more seasoned psychologist. He was prepared to begin a successful forensic practice at once.

Invite protégés to participate with you in various dimensions of your professional life. The best mentors understand that protégés need to watch them perform the activities necessary in a particular field. They appreciate the fact that some complex professional behaviors (e.g., writing a grant, running a meeting, or pitching a proposal to a client) can only be learned by observation. In some settings, the code of professional conduct is largely tacit and unspoken—requiring the mentor to quietly teach and demonstrate the art of communication and success in a world largely foreign to the protégé. Protégés are usually eager to accept opportunities to observe and participate with their mentors in the daily minutia of "being" a professional. In any organization, effective mentors are engaged with their protégés, first teaching, and then showing their protégés how to do business. Mentors prompt protégés to watch, practice under the mentor's supervision, and then practice independently.

Excellent mentors intentionally model ethical behavior and professional responsibility. Ironically, protégés will learn ethical behavior from the mentor regardless of the degree to which the mentor is intentional about modeling in this domain. Implicit attitudes and explicit behavior communicate more to the protégé than any lecture the mentor might offer. The mentor must be fair, just, and honest in dealings with colleagues, superiors, clients, and the protégé. It is imperative that mentors appreciate the extent to which they are accorded *idealized influence* in the lives of their protégés. Mentors are viewed as trustworthy symbols of success and accomplishment. Regardless of merit, they will become objects of admiration, idealization, emulation, and respect. Fine mentors accept the power accorded role models and use it to intentionally model ethical professionalism.

The professional life of the mentor is played out before the protégé. As a model, the mentor assists the protégé in forging a professional identity. A healthy identity allows for imperfections as well as personal strengths. This means accepting oneself as a professional and a person and refusing to feign omnipotence, omniscience, or perfection. Mentors bear some responsibility for modeling humility, health, and the integration of professional and personal roles. Research indicates that female protégés are particularly drawn to mentors who model successfully the management of their professional and personal lives.

Key Components

- *Invite protégés to participate in various aspects of your professional life.*
- *Understand that some professional tasks can only be learned through direct observation.*
- *Accept the idealized influence you hold in relation to your protégés and use it to model excellence and ethical conduct.*
- *Allow protégés to observe at first, but require increasing participation and engagement.*
- *Model humility, health, and integration of personal and professional roles.*

19
Display Dependability

Charles was a remarkably successful executive director of a large education research institute. Relatively young for someone in his position, he had achieved much through talent, tenacity, and excellent management skills. When Clara took a position as a new project manager with the institute, Charles recognized her as someone with great potential. He began to mentor her and learned that she had interest in an eventual managerial leadership position. The two discussed her ideal career trajectory and the various tasks and positions Clara would need assistance attaining on her way up. During the second year of the mentorship, Charles was inundated with speaking invitations, book offers, and even a request to lead a presidential education initiative. Although he found his schedule becoming absurdly packed, and although he decided he would have to scale back on some of his duties and commitments at work, he was careful to follow-through with the biweekly meetings he had scheduled for Clara, as well as impromptu conversations about her career. He continued to review drafts of her research carefully and return them expeditiously. As a result, Charles's opportunities and popularity only benefited Clara. She always found him dependable and this significantly bolstered her sense of value and confidence.

When it comes to being a mentor, talk is cheap. It is delightful to begin interacting with a talented and admiring junior. It is harder to follow-through with the real work of mentoring. Excellent mentoring demands consistency and reliability; it occasionally requires self-sacrifice. Yet, dependability is a cornerstone of mentoring. To say it bluntly: put your time where your mouth is or do not commit to mentorships.

In a survey of several hundred university graduate students regarding the traits they most wanted in a mentor, one of the top-rated preferences was dependability. The specific item rated highly by students read: "can always be counted on to follow-through when he/she makes a commitment." The message here is loud and clear. Protégés want consistency, dependability, and follow through—not words but action. Good intentions mean little when they are not backed up by behavior.

So how do mentors demonstrate dependability? First, they stay true to the agreements and commitments made early in the mentorship. Perhaps the simplest yet most often violated corollary of this rule is: attend all scheduled meetings and activities with protégés—don't forget and don't be late. If you have promised to provide specific mentoring functions, or to help the protégé achieve a specific milestone, follow through. Second, mentors should ensure a reasonable turn-around time. One of the most frequent complaints given by protégés is that mentors fail to return drafts of reports, proposals, or scholarly work in a timely fashion. If one of your essential avenues for teaching and coaching is reviewing your protégé's work, then do it expeditiously. Otherwise the protégé languishes and professional development slows. Sometimes, dependability is communicated simply by speed! Third, mentors need to be emotionally consistent. Nothing destabilizes and diminishes a mentorship faster than an emotionally unpredictable or over-reactive mentor. Finally, mentors should avoid the "inspiration only" trap. The mentor who generates creative ideas and collaborative possibilities but fails to follow through is unreliable. The protégé learns not to take this mentor's promises seriously.

There is a dark side to mentor unreliability. When a mentor makes promises and plans with a protégé, but fails to follow through, protégés must interpret the reason for this disconnect between word and deed. Protégés might conclude that they are a failure, a disappointment, an unimportant entity, or perhaps guilty of causing the mentor to be angry. Certainly, these conclusions are erroneous. Nevertheless, they obviously are corrosive to protégés' self-esteem and confidence. In sum, the unreliable and inconsistent mentor can ultimately leave the protégé worse off in terms of professional confidence and identity. This is unacceptable.

Here is a final paradox for mentors to consider. The most powerful, accomplished, and successful professionals are the very ones who are most vulnerable to being scattered, harried, and unreliable in the mentor role. Successful professionals are in demand. In a malaise of overwhelming demands and overextended schedules, a mentor is tempted to rush, cut corners, and economize when it comes to protégés. Refusing to shortchange a protégé may be one of the most salient traits of an excellent mentor.

Key Components

- *Make following through with commitments to your protégé a top priority.*
- *Provide your protégé with expeditious turn-around and feedback when reviewing his or her work.*
- *Work at emotional stability and consistency. Don't overreact.*
- *Refuse to cut-corners when it comes to allocating time to your protégé.*

Traits of
Excellent Mentors

Matters of Style and Personality

Having explored the skills of excellent mentors, it is essential now for us to take a closer look at the person of the mentor. In this section of *The Elements*, we consider the key components of *being* the sort of person to whom protégés are most attracted and find most helpful. These are the elements bearing on personality and interpersonal style. The important questions are these: (a) What are you like interpersonally? (b) What are your primary relational habits? and (c) How does it feel for a protégé to be in relationship with you?

Although a wide range of personality features can be found among good mentors (e.g., some are socially introverted while others savor plenty of group interaction; some are compulsively organized while others prefer spontaneity and last-minute planning), there are some personality features and interpersonal qualities that typically contribute to successful mentoring. Protégés, like other human beings, are naturally drawn to and often helped by mentors who are warm, good listeners, and unconditionally accepting. Protégés also prefer mentors who are trustworthy, interpersonally sensitive, respectful of values, and able to use and appreciate humor.

In this section, we consider the personal qualities and characteristics that matter in successful mentoring. Although interpersonal elements may be more difficult to modify and develop than the previously discussed mentoring functions, all mentors can improve and polish their interpersonal approach. Keep in mind that the important elements in this section have much to do with the real *art* of mentoring.

20
Exude Warmth

As a new junior editor for a medium-sized publishing house, Roger was drawn to Frank—one of the senior book editors. Not only was Frank an accomplished editor and well-liked member of the company, he was also gifted in how he related to people. Co-workers in the office readily took to him. Roger noticed that Frank always made him feel good about himself when the two had a conversation or encounter with each other. It was hard for Roger to put his finger precisely on what happened when they were together, but he was certain about one thing: Frank made him feel special and valued. Actually, Frank possessed a number of favorable qualities. He was kind, genuine, and laughed and smiled easily. He was free with complimentary and supportive comments (e.g., "I can't believe how lucky we are to have you here Roger. You're a delight to work with"). Frank took the time to inquire about Roger's family and his experience thus far on the job. In Frank's presence, Roger felt like he was ten feet tall.

Like a seed that needs nourishing to germinate and grow, people need the proper ingredients in their environments to flourish. An important ingredient for growth in a mentorship is emotional warmth. Protégés in all arenas rate mentor warmth and caring as among the most important mentor traits. Warmth is an attitude of friendliness, approachability, and openness. When mentors radiate warmth, protégés can bask in that emotional sunlight. Warmth translates into respect and being nonjudgmental. Protégés in warm mentorships report feeling accepted, prized, and admired. Mentor warmth charges the mentorship with positive emotional valence. This is because human beings are drawn to warmth, whether it is physical or psychological.

Warmth has verbal and nonverbal components, and you cannot have one without the other. Warmth is communicated verbally through affirming comments (e.g., "You are a delight to supervise."), expressions of concern (e.g., "You seem to be sluggish of late. Are you getting enough rest?"), and statements of appreciation (e.g., "I am so thankful you found the error in the data set."). But to really have impact, these verbal expressions also must be sincere. Sincerity is communicated nonverbally through attentiveness, good eye contact, a soothing tone, kind facial expressions, open and relaxed body posture, and physical touch. Sometimes a simple touch to the arm or pat on the back may say more than a thousand words. Mentors should just be careful not to cross acceptable boundaries of physical contact.

The opposite of this quality is emotional coolness. Mentors cut of this fabric are destined to seriously limit the value of their relationships with protégés. Under their tutelage, protégés do not feel safe, respected, or cared about. In all likelihood, protégés will not flourish or reach their full potential. Instead, they will use much of their energy staying on guard and trying to figure out where they stand with their mentor rather than putting it to productive use.

Emotional coolness comes from two primary sources. Some mentors are simply detached and insulated. This is their core personality, which represents their defense against pain and trauma. At some level, they just decide that it is not worth the risk of making themselves vulnerable to other people. Cool mentors are difficult to change. Other mentors may have the capacity for warmth but lack the requisite skills for expressing warmth to protégés. A more promising scenario, these mentors simply need to learn and practice the skills of interpersonal attentiveness, kindness, and emotional availability. By learning from good models and taking the time to practice methods of conveying warmth, most mentors can improve their skills in this area.

Key Components

- *Recognize warmth as a necessary condition for maximal protégé growth and development.*
- *Radiate warmth with an attitude of friendliness, approachability, and kindness.*
- *Consistently offer verbal and nonverbal expressions of sincere interest, thorough acceptance, and genuine positive regard.*

21
Listen Actively

When Linda reflected on her mentorship with Megan, specifically why Megan became such an important figure in her life, she often returned to a recurring experience: sitting in Megan's office and describing a problem or idea while her mentor sat carefully listening to every word. As a senior vice-president in a multinational financial institution, Megan's days were crowded to say the least. She still recognized Linda's talents and was committed to guiding her through the ranks of management. Megan demonstrated her commitment through deliberate and focused listening whenever Linda approached her with a question, idea, or concern. On these occasions, Megan would come around her desk, sit in a chair across from Linda, lean forward, and show attentiveness before thoughtfully responding. Linda knew Megan heard every word because her responses showed a clear grasp of the concern or creative notion. Megan's intentional and skillful listening conveyed a powerful message: You are very important and well worth this expenditure of time and energy.

Most people can hear words but not everyone takes the time to listen. Listening is more than hearing. It is active attention to two levels of communication: (a) the *overt message*—the literal or concrete meaning of spoken words; and (b) the *covert message*—the more subtle or implied meaning. It is essential that you deliberately work at "hearing" your protégé on both levels. At times, incongruence between the overt and covert messages will offer clues to the protégé's real experience.

Protégés rank active listening high among the traits of ideal mentors. Unfortunately, poor listening is an epidemic in western culture. People do not take the time to attend to the meanings behind other people's words. Even in supervision and management, mentors often rush to give an answer, offer advice, or tell their story without tuning in to their protégés' real concern or point of view. This inattentiveness communicates that what the protégé has to say is not worthwhile or important.

Active listening is actually a complex and demanding activity, consisting of several microskills. Here are several that should be especially useful for mentors. Use good nonverbal responses (e.g., nodding, maintaining eye contact, smiling), and make sure these are commensurate with your verbal responses. Use verbal prompts to encourage protégés to express themselves as fully as possible (e.g., "yes, umhm, tell me more about that"). Do not interrupt. Interruptions make protégés feel that what they have to say is not important. Ask for clarity about vague comments. This shows protégés that they are being taken seriously. Accurately reflect what protégés communicate. Reflection means to paraphrase or summarize the core themes of the protégé's message; accurate reflection is much harder than you might think! This shows that protégés are being understood.

Key Components

- *Drop other activities when protégés want to talk; give them your undivided attention.*
- *Listen to identify both overt and covert meanings in your protégé's communication.*
- *Ensure congruence between your verbal and nonverbal demeanor; communicate genuine interest and consistent attention.*
- *Reflect (accurately paraphrase) your protégé's primary concerns.*

22
Show Unconditional Regard

When Louise began to mentor Jamal, a college sophomore, she was impressed by his intelligence and promise as a writer. As an English professor with many years of experience, she also recognized Jamal's ambivalence about college, his own ability, and his life and career aspirations. As a mentor, Louise tirelessly encouraged Jamal to write and praised his efforts. She sponsored his short stories for publication and listened carefully to his concerns and hopes. After Jamal briefly dropped out of college, then changed his major, she nevertheless continued to ask him to take "coffee breaks" in the campus grill, praised his talents, and expressed genuine interest in his life and career. Anticipating rejection, Jamal was surprised by his mentor's consistent high regard of him. Although he did not graduate with a major in English, he did begin to write successfully, and later attributed much of his success to Louise.

Many achievements in life are based on meeting some predetermined conditions. As the saying goes, "There is no such thing as a free lunch." Homeowners must qualify financially to get a mortgage. Attorneys must pass the bar exam to practice law. And track stars have to run faster than their competitors to win a race.

While mentors have lofty expectations of protégés, there is one area where no conditions should be set: The acceptance of protégés as people and unique individuals. Famous psychologist Carl Rogers championed this idea of unconditional positive regard—a prime ingredient in the process of positive growth and change. He described this ingredient in such terms as acceptance, nonpossessive caring, and prizing. Mentors demonstrate unconditional regard when they patiently listen, communicate authentic interest, and accept the protégé even when the protégé errs or fails. In fact, a mentor's unconditional regard is most apparent when a protégé fails. For not even failure earns the protégé the mentor's disregard. Instead, the mentor's message is clear: This mistake or bad outcome does not define who you are. Ideal mentors not only hold positive attitudes about their protégés, they express this regard through what they say and how they behave.

Unconditional positive regard has several key components. First, the mentor must communicate an unquestionable commitment to work with the protégé and a freely chosen willingness to do so. More than this, however, the mentor must communicate that the decision to mentor is based on high regard for the protégé's fundamental virtues and extraordinary promise. Commitment is tangibly expressed when the mentor schedules time for the protégé, faithfully keeps appointments, and carefully maintains confidentiality. Of these expressions, scheduling time exclusively for the protégé is particularly imperative. Interactions based only on hurried hallway chats or side conversations during larger meetings convey disregard. Perhaps the greatest damage is done by mentors who are incongruent. They verbalize their commitments to protégés but disregard them by their actions. Here their actions speak louder than their words.

Second, unconditional regard is communicated through diligent efforts to understand the protégé. Excellent mentors work at understanding their protégé's point of view and communicate this understanding by asking clarifying questions and avoiding the tendency to superimpose themselves on the protégé. Finally, unconditional positive regard requires a nonjudgmental attitude. An effective mentor suspends judgment of a protégé's thoughts, feelings, and actions. Instead, the mentor accepts them and works to help the protégé understand how each might influence achievement of his or her personal and professional dreams.

Key Components

- *Regard your protégés as fundamentally and unconditionally good and worthwhile.*
- *Demonstrate consistent acceptance, nonpossessive caring, and even prizing.*
- *Show unconditional positive regard even when protégés fail.*
- *Demonstrate positive regard through commitment of time and resources and efforts at genuine understanding.*
- *Be nonjudgmental and understanding of protégé thoughts, feelings, and actions.*

23
Tolerate Idealization

Fresh from the Naval Academy and a newly minted Ensign, Brett stood in awe of his first department head, Commander Creighton. Not only was the commander a veteran of naval combat, the recipient of numerous awards, and a shoe-in for eventual promotion to admiral, he was also an inspiring leader. He was poised, articulate, interpersonally savvy, and intellectually sharp. In addition, Commander Creighton showed interest in Brett and began to offer advice and challenge. Although Brett was initially nervous, befuddled, and practically worshipped his boss, Commander Creighton remained kind, humble, and tolerant. He understood that Brett's reverence was a necessary early step in their mentorship. He further understood that attempting to pop Brett's bubble by airing his human weaknesses and imperfections was unlikely to assist Brett's development. Over time, in the context of a strong mentorship, Brett's idealism was tempered by a more reality-based picture of his mentor. Still, he deeply admired many of the commander's techniques and traits and adopted many of these in his own leadership style. Later, when the two had gone their separate ways, an astute observer would note that although Brett manifested many of Commander

Creighton's characteristics, he expressed these uniquely, in a professional style that had become his own.

After ducklings are hatched, they enter a short but critical period of development. They identify a parent and proceed to mimic and model each of this parent's behaviors. They follow this parent everywhere and never let her out of sight. This *imprinting* process is instinctual and crucial for survival. Imprinting also occurs in humans. Children idealize their parents. The good father smiles, but understands not to chasten the fawning son who insists upon accompanying him everywhere, mimicking his behaviors and expressions, and generally getting underfoot. Something tells the father that this is essential. The wisest parents enjoy this stage while it lasts.

Protégés may need to idealize their mentors early in the relationship. Initially it can be the gateway to healthy identification, but idealization poses some significant problems if protégés get stuck there. After identification, protégés can move to individuation as a mature and separate professional. For this process to unfold, mentors must learn to gracefully tolerate protégé idealization.

Idealization is a normal developmental process. We all go through it several times during our lives. Idealization involves finding characteristics we do not possess but observe in others—characteristics we admire and wish to develop or discover. Idealization is the necessary process by which we locate and identify those things we want to become. Idealization fosters growth and empowers us. As young children, we typically idealize parents or important caregivers. Literal and figurative giants of strength, power, and virtue, there is much in a parent for the young person to idealize. Later, as adolescents and young adults, we idealize others with whom we relate. These idealized others serve as templates for our ambition. A competent and accomplished mentor is the perfect person to fit the bill. Protégés need to admire and idealize the mentor. They need to look upon the mentor's traits, skills, and polished mannerisms through rose-colored lenses. Like the ducklings, they need that critical period of waddling behind their mentor. Mentors should not be put off by this behavior. If they do their jobs right, it won't last forever.

Although idealization helps to motivate a protégé to enter a mentorship, it subsides and is ideally replaced by something else—*identification.*

Less idealistic and biased, identification reflects the degree to which the protégé wants to be like the mentor. It is an important process whereby aspects of the idealized are internalized and become the protégé's own. A crucial developmental task for the protégé, identification is a process of integrating various identifications into a coherent individual identity. In effect, the protégé uses initial idealization to identify desirable characteristics and form a personal sense of self. What begins as idealized excitement and awe at the outset of a mentorship can evolve into internalized goals and ambitions. The protégé takes what he or she needs from the mentor to craft a professional identity and eventually individuate.

Here is the crucial piece for mentors: gracefully recognize and tolerate idealization—it is a core feature of good mentoring and the protégé needs the mentor to allow it to occur. You may be uncomfortable with adulation, but keep in mind that this is really not about you. It is about professional neophytes working to clarify who they will become. Be honored yet humble when idealized. Your protégé needs permission to "imprint": to waddle along proudly in your shadow for a period of time. Later, idealization will be less urgent and more realistic—paving the way for healthy identification of those traits the protégé most wishes to emulate. If tolerated well, idealization will allow your protégé to move from clone to colleague. That is the goal.

Key Components

- *Accept the fact that your protégé needs to initially see you through idealized lenses.*
- *Tolerate idealization and adulation with grace and humility.*
- *Remember that idealization turns to identification and that identification is crucial for professional identity development.*
- *As your protégé matures, he or she can see you in a more balanced and realistic way.*

24
Embrace Humor

A fifteen-year veteran of Congressman Smith's staff and an excellent and energetic aide, Joe immediately appealed to Bonnie as a potential mentor. Not only

*was Joe quick to help Bonnie learn the ropes around the office, he was kind, sup-
portive, and genuinely interested in helping Bonnie succeed. Joe also had a good
sense of humor that he frequently used to help Bonnie take the edge off of her tendency to exaggerate her mistakes and punish herself for perceived shortcomings.
When Bonnie began to do so, Joe would often lower his voice conspiratorially,
frown, and say something like "yes Bonnie, your mistake will probably cost the
congressman his career. Not only that, it may cause a downturn in the economy,
lead to a new world war, and send the globe into chaos. Thanks a lot Bonnie."
Bonnie not only laughed, she quickly recognized her fruitless tendency toward
self-criticism.*

Nothing can take the place of a good laugh. Laughter is a soothing
balm—medicine to the soul. Perhaps, this is why protégés rank humor as
one of the five top traits of ideal mentors. A mentor with a knack for good
humor is often perceived as fully human, approachable, and fun to be
around. In the anxiety-ridden world of neophyte protégés, humor serves
several important functions: It normalizes the experiences of protégés,
minimizes their fears, and reminds them that few things in life are really
catastrophic.

One of the best uses of humor in a mentorship is in helping protégés
not take themselves too seriously. How often have we seen protégés place
ridiculous demands on themselves (e.g., "I must make a brilliant presentation at the staff meeting," or "If I don't get this report done precisely
when I promised, it will prove I'm an idiot")? These types of demands obviously are absurd. For protégés in such a state of irrationality, a humorous challenge such as a *paradoxical intention* might be just the trick:
"You're right, it would be absolutely awful if you didn't speak perfectly at
the meeting. In fact, it's the worst thing I can imagine. Both of us would
probably be finished with our careers and end up on the streets."

Humor can also diminish anxiety about the realities of life and career.
Life is hard and so is work. The possibility of failure in either is real.
Therefore, protégés cannot afford to take them lightly. But they cannot
take themselves so seriously that work and play are artificially divorced.
The good mentor helps his or her protégé learn how to moderate serious
business with humor, how to mix career with play. Sometimes the best
thing mentors can do is to use humor and make light of themselves.

Everyone has "blown it" and stumbled along the way. When mentors can be light hearted about some of their mistakes (both historic and present), they indirectly encourage their protégés. Research indicates that protégés are drawn to "down-to-earth" mentors, those who can fall flat and get up laughing. But remember, humor can have a downside.

Used inappropriately, humor can be counterproductive, even harmful. This is especially true when mentors use humor to belittle a protégé or trivialize important matters. When humor gratifies a mentor without edifying the protégé, something is wrong. Also, some protégés have little capacity for humor and respond poorly to humorous interventions even when they are well intended and nicely delivered. Excellent mentors read protégés accurately and use humor only when protégés are receptive.

Key Components

- *Laugh at yourself often as a means of modeling humility and perspective.*
- *Use humor to help protégés take themselves less seriously.*
- *Teach protégés to mix work and laughter.*
- *Avoid using humor to belittle protégés or trivialize matters important to them.*

25
Do Not Expect Perfection

As a new brokerage trainee, Joel often felt like an "imposter." He was relieved when Tricia, a more experienced broker, began offering him advice, coaching, and reassurance. Tricia became concerned, however, when she noticed Joel frequently pulled "all-nighters" to complete projects, refused to bring reports to closure until he believed they were error-free, and appeared full of shame and humiliation whenever an error or discrepancy was noted in something he wrote or reported. Tricia began to gently but consistently confront Joel's perfectionistic behavior by saying things like, "Joel, I know you're trying to do good work here, and you are. But perfection is unattainable so I'm asking you to stop striving for that. You look tired and unhappy. Does your demanding perfection improve your work or your mood?" Over time, she also shared some of her own strategies for developing reasonable goals and helped Joel to make light of minor errors and imperfections.

No one is perfect—not even the brightest and the best. As the old saying goes, "to err is human." Therefore, mentors always should expect excellence, but not even for a moment should they send the wrong message that a protégé should be perfect. Much of what disturbs protégés involves their unrealistic and perfectionistic attitudes about life, work, and themselves. Psychologist Thomas Lorch says "A perfectionist is motivated by a fear of failure and a sense of duty rather than enthusiasm for the creative process."

Perfectionism often stems from early life experiences. Perfectionistic protégés often hail from environments that promulgate a "zero-defect" attitude about performance. In adulthood, perceived shortcomings are cause for severe self-recrimination and protégés will expect similar intolerance and rejection from mentors. The net effect of perfectionism is diminished enjoyment of work and life.

Competent mentors communicate a vision of the protégé as human. Sure protégés are gifted and talented, but mentors also see their shortcomings and accept them as imperfect. And in the words of David Burns, mentors understand that perfectionism is a "script for self-defeat." For these reasons, the excellent mentor is cautious about communicating, intentionally or not, expectations for perfect performance. They discern the difference between high expectation and inhuman demand. Although some perfectionistic communication is overt (e.g., "now do it again and this time get it perfect"), the more common and destructive messages to protégés are insidious and subtle. For example, a derisive shake of the head or rolling of the eyes may tell protégés much more about your requirements of them than all of your verbal reassurances combined.

To send the right message, mentors demonstrate comfort with their own limitations. They can self-disclose, for example, letting protégés know about their insecurities and overwhelming feelings when learning the vocation. They do not hesitate to utter the words "I don't know" when they cannot answer a question or lack knowledge in one area. When protégés require extra time or make mistakes, they seize the opportunity to provide guidance and correction. Although they do not avoid confronting mediocre effort or pointing out errors and poor performance, they manage to simultaneously convey patience, tolerance, and an abiding expectation that the protégé will rise to the mentor's challenge for excellence.

Key Components

- *Expect excellence without perfection.*
- *Help protégés discern the dysfunctional nature of perfectionistic attitudes and beliefs.*
- *Avoid subtle or nonverbal as well as overt messages that perfection is required.*
- *Serve as an intentional and transparent model of imperfect excellence.*

26
Attend to Interpersonal Cues

Chris often marveled at his mentor's "way with people." A professor in Chris's MBA program, Dom had become Chris's mentor when it became clear the two shared several interests and when Chris expressed interest in earning a PhD. Dom was one of the few people who could really "read" Chris's emotions and worries before Chris said a word. Dom was a master at accurately identifying both his own feelings ("Chris, I have to tell you, not getting that grant has left me feeling depressed today"), and those of others ("Chris, you look anxious. Should we talk about it?"). It seemed to Chris that Dom was able to tailor his demeanor and approach to "fit" Chris's mood and his specific mentoring needs.

If given a choice, most protégés would prefer a mentor who has keen interpersonal competence over one who has a powerful intellect. In other words, exceptional mentoring is about much more than IQ. Psychologist and renowned author Daniel Goleman uses the phrase *emotional intelligence* to convey the importance of relating competently to others. In addition to their warmth, active listening, and sympathy, interpersonally competent mentors "read" relational cues and use their reading to maximize the health and productivity of the relationship. These mentors are naturally kind, competent, and fun to be around. They exude competence and confidence in the emotional realm. For these reasons, they are sought out by protégés for guidance and advice.

Several distinct skills characterize *emotionally intelligent* mentors. First, they are self-aware. They understand their own psychological dynamics—their moods, emotions, and drives and they understand how these affect other people. Second, they have self-control. They experience the full range of human emotions, but when disappointment sets in, they do not become depressively dependent, and when frustrated, they do not become volcanically enraged. Instead, they can share their disappointment in a way that is constructive. Third, they tune into the emotional make-up of other people. They successfully read verbal and nonverbal cues. Because of this skill, they often are effective as cross-cultural mentors. Fourth, they are proficient in building social networks. Not only can they find common ground and build rapport with protégés, they do so with colleagues and superiors as well. As a result of their friendliness and interpersonal savvy, they have the knack for positively impacting people and constructing alliances that ultimately benefit both themselves and their protégés (e.g., protégés have access to a broader range of connections and associates).

Emotional intelligence may be one of the most underrated and unexplored characteristics of great mentors. To prove the point, observe traffic flow patterns of mentoring in any organization. Typically you will see protégés flocking to prospective mentors with proven skills on the emotional/interpersonal plane. Experience shows and research supports the principle that protégés are drawn to emotionally skilled mentors.

Key Components

- *Pay attention to your own emotional life and demonstrate emotional self-awareness.*
- *Model a range of appropriate human emotions without expressing emotion impulsively or destructively.*
- *Work at accurate understanding of the emotional states of protégés.*
- *Use kindness, interpersonal savvy, and emotional awareness to build professional relationships. These will benefit your protégés.*

27
Be Trustworthy

Art's integrity was one of the things Aaron most respected about his mentor. Art was always honest, dependable, and known around the engineering firm as a re-

liable and "up-front" guy. For this reason, Aaron felt nervous but not over-whelmed when he admitted his amphetamine addiction to Art. Although accept-ing, kind, and respectful, Art told Aaron in clear terms that he would be required to enter treatment, that Art would keep Aaron's disclosure private (only those in management with a legitimate need to know would be involved), and that while he would support Aaron fervently, he would also recommend termination if Aaron's addiction interfered with his performance over time or if he continued to use substances and placed the company or others at risk. Aaron's trust in Art was reaffirmed by this experience.

Ideal mentors are trustworthy. They mean what they say and say what they mean, creating a safe and reliable haven for protégés. Trust might be described as protégés' perception that mentors will not mislead or hurt them. Because of a mentor's status and reputation, a certain amount of trust is automatically accorded the mentor. As the mentorship matures, trust is earned. The mentor must demonstrate through unwavering consistency that he or she is worthy of the protégé's continued trust.

Mentors garner trustworthiness through several avenues. One avenue is through their integrity or fidelity. Fidelity involves honesty and promise-keeping in relation to others and to broader organizations. Not only does the trustworthy mentor carefully adhere to codes of legal and ethical conduct, the mentor is fundamentally committed to internalized moral principles and strives to be a person of virtue and moral character. Because it is impossible for mentors to anticipate every moral or ethical quandary they will encounter, they are faithful to undergirding moral principles such as care and justice and always place the welfare of those who depend upon them (protégés) before their own needs and interests. Interestingly, mentors are perceived as trustworthy when they honestly acknowledge and confront protégé's mistakes or bad behavior. Caring enough to confront enhances the protégé's sense of trust. Finally, mentors express fidelity by monitoring themselves and their own mentoring behavior, ensuring healthy and respectful interactions with those they mentor.

Mentors also generate trust through genuineness. Their words, actions, and feelings are consistent and transparent. Genuine mentors adhere to the same time-honored principles and values regardless of the situation or who is observing them. What you see with these mentors is what you get. They do not play on their one-up position and from the highest-level person to the lowest-level person in the organization, they always show respect.

To find out what a mentor is really made of, protégés sometimes put the trustworthiness of a mentor to the test. Here it is imperative for mentors to get a passing grade. One protégé may confide in the mentor a deeply held secret or private disclosure. This protégé really wants to know if the mentor can maintain confidentiality. Another protégé may request of the mentor additional time or assistance. This protégé really wants to know if he or she is as important as the mentor claims. At times, a protégé will share a failure or shortcoming. This protégé wants to see if the mentor is unconditionally accepting. Finally, a protégé may deliver unsatisfactory work. He or she may be testing the mentor's requirements for exceptional effort.

Key Components

- *Demonstrate trustworthiness with consistency, reliability, and integrity.*
- *Keep promises to protégés.*
- *Adhere to professional and organizational codes.*
- *Honestly confront problems, mistakes, and shortcomings.*
- *Ensure congruence in word and deed.*
- *Maintain confidence and protect protégé disclosures.*

28
Respect Values

One of the fastest advancing young executives in the history of the company, Connie understood how difficult it was for women to climb the ladder in a male-dominated corporation. As vice president for operations, Connie was in a powerful position to develop other women aspiring to make the climb. She became impressed with Brinnell, a junior manager in her division. Brinnell was bright, energetic, and obviously impressed with Connie. Before long, Connie had taken an interest in Brinnell. The two of them began working closely on some projects.

They enjoyed frequent discussions designed to prepare Brinnell for success and advancement. Soon, however, Connie became frustrated with Brinnell's active planning for her marriage the following spring and mentioning of the possibility of having children. Although she had hobbies and good friends, Connie placed little value on marriage or family and felt that these might inhibit a successful career for a woman. Aware of the value difference between them, Connie acknowledged this to Brinnell and even made light of her own tendency to place work before romantic or family interests. She then worked at supporting Brinnell without coercing her to alter her main value commitments—recognizing and accepting that Brinnell's career trajectory may diverge from her own.

Shared values undergird strong relationships. We are drawn to people that share our sense of right and wrong, our sense of justice, and our beliefs about the things we deem important in life. People are attracted to others who have similar values. Not surprisingly, great mentor–protégé pairs often value similar ideas and commitments. Even when values are discordant at the outset of mentoring, we find that values shift over time so that mentor and protégé values become more congruent. Of course, we think it is the protégé, not the mentor whose values should change. One of the great paradoxes of mentoring is that while great mentors understand and respect protégés' value differences, protégé values often shift over time to better match those of the mentor, and further, the better the value match, the better the mentoring outcomes and the closer the mentoring bond.

When protégé values (ethical/moral, societal, religious) shift to more closely approximate those of the mentor, we call this values *conversion* or values *assimilation*. It seems to be an inevitable outcome whenever an impressionable protégé in any field works closely with an admired and successful mentor. Protégés adopt the behaviors, professional practices, and over time, the values of an influential mentor. Although experts may caution mentors to be "value neutral" in dealings with protégés, we assert that this is an improbable stance. Protégés inevitably will become aware of the mentor's values on important issues no matter how much the mentor strives for neutrality. Therefore, "neutrality" is neither realistic nor desirable. It is preferable that protégés see the mentor's value positions without feeling coerced to adopt them. This stance requires mentors to be constantly vigilant regarding their own needs for agreement from subordinates and conscious of their influential position with protégés.

So how do some mentors go wrong when it comes to protégé values? There are several ways that mentors can be disrespectful of protégés in this regard. First, mentors can attempt to interfere with the freedom of protégés to choose their own values. They make approval, protection, or continuation of mentoring contingent upon adopting the mentor's values. Second, mentors can intentionally impose their own values on to protégés, which is a form of coercion. Third, mentors can become judgmental or moralistic. They may condemn the character of the protégé for failing to adopt or agree with the mentor's values. Fourth, mentors can be propagandizing. They may handle value issues in a biased manner. This action communicates to protégés that only certain options regarding values are healthy or valid in the eyes of the mentor. Finally, mentors can use subtle coercion. They may use selective reinforcement (nodding, smiling or verbally affirming only when the protégé voices value perspectives that match the mentor's own). Such coercion may occur without the mentor being consciously aware.

Key Components

- *Understand that the "pressure" is on your protégé to shift values in the direction of your own.*
- *Do not pretend to be value "neutral." Acknowledge your core beliefs and values.*
- *Respect your protégé's values and work to avoid direct values conversion through coercion or propagandizing.*
- *Acknowledge and discuss value differences when appropriate.*

29
Do Not Stoop to Jealousy

As Larry's mentorship with Yolanda progressed, he became increasingly aware of her unusual talent as a researcher and writer. A PhD candidate in Biology, Yolanda began publishing single-authored articles in major journals. Initially

threatened by his protégé's success, Larry quickly realized the need to uncondi-
tionally and actively support Yolanda. To that end he praised her successes and
urged her on. He even encouraged the development of a secondary mentorship
with an African American woman who was a scholar in another graduate de-
partment on campus. He did so because Yolanda had expressed feelings of racial
alienation in the all-white Biology department.

Some circumstances remind mentors of their limitations. One important reminder is when protégés show talents and gifts that surpass their mentors. Another important reminder is when their protégés benefit from other mentorships. Instead of becoming jealous, mentors should celebrate their protégés gifts and opportunities. They should encourage protégés to develop *mentoring constellations* or networks. Such a constellation typically consists of one primary mentorship as well as secondary mentorships. Secondary mentorships are typically shorter in duration, are characterized by less emotional bonding than a primary mentorship, and focus on specific functions such as learning the ropes in a new specialty area. Protégés sometimes seek secondary mentors to fulfill needs that cannot be met in the primary mentorship. They may seek out someone with specialized knowledge or expertise that the primary mentor does not have. They may seek out someone of their race, gender, or religious faith who can identify with their unique cultural and emotional challenges. Protégés sometimes benefit both from peer mentorships where there is greater mutuality, emotional support, and friendship or they benefit from relationships with senior personnel in other departments or professionals in other organizations.

It is never in the best interest of anyone for mentors to become jealous, possessive, or territorial. If they become jealous, the message to protégés goes something like this: This is a safe and helpful relationship only so long as you don't become too successful or autonomous. This reaction places protégés in a double bind and compromises their potential for maximal development. Protégés of jealous mentors may sabotage or cover-up evidence of their own growth and success. These protégés are forced to make a painful choice: downplaying themselves to protect the mentor's ego or fully actualizing themselves at the expense of garnering the mentor's support. Neither choice is desirable.

Jealousy, paradoxically, is detrimental to mentors themselves. Jealous mentors force healthy protégés to leave the relationship or produce below their capabilities. In either scenario, the potential returns and benefits to the mentor are lost.

To counter this reaction, mentors should explore the causes of their jealousy, work diligently to put their feelings in check, and place the protégé's welfare above their own needs for affection, friendship, and adulation. In human relationships, jealousy signals perceived threat. Jealous reactions are self-protective; they are designed to shield oneself from the threat of ego wounding. Jealous mentors find their egos endangered by protégés who achieve beyond their own capacity, and by protégés who no longer depend on them as they did earlier in the relationship. Mentors should use their jealousy to serve as a red flag that they have lost sight of their primary purpose. Finally, they should use their jealousy to determine if their reaction reflects an unhealthy emotional involvement with the protégé.

Key Concepts

- *Remember that jealousy undermines mentoring and nearly always signals your own fear and insecurity.*
- *Use jealous feelings to re-orient to the purpose of mentoring: the protégé's development.*
- *Encourage protégé autonomy and celebrate protégé success.*
- *Encourage secondary mentorships to maximize protégé growth.*

Arranging the Mentor–Protégé Relationship

Matters of Beginning

One of our prime motivations for writing *The Elements* is to help our readers avoid becoming *incidental* mentors—professionals who stumble into the role without forethought or deliberate consideration. Instead, we encourage our readers to become *intentional* mentors—professionals who deliberately select protégés and carefully manage the development and course of mentorships.

In this section of *The Elements,* we discuss the all-important process of intentionally arranging a good mentorship. It should be obvious that this process always begins with the selection of protégés. CEOs, graduate school faculty, and marriage partners the world over know that a good "match" is everything when it comes to finding successful employees, students, or partners. Successful mentors choose protégés they can be reasonably certain of effectively mentoring. In addition to the concern about compatibility, mentors must ensure that new mentorships are well structured. Protégés must be given clear expectations, relational boundaries must be established, and both parties must have some appreciation of the potential risks and benefits of entering into the relationship. When mentorships involve mentors and protégés of different genders or races, these differences should be sensitively considered. When necessary, these differences should be discussed early in the relationship. The open discussion, as well as the willingness to work through the concerns of similarities, differences, expectations, and relationship contours, helps to put the relationship on a productive path.

It may seem like a paradox, but from the outset, excellent mentors plan for development, change, and even ending a mentorship. Mentors must take a long-term perspective on the relationship from the start. The responsibility for the evaluation of the relationship certainly cannot be placed on the shoulders of protégés. Rather mentors must plan for the protégé's increasing independence and, at some point, termination of the formal mentorship. During the formal period of mentorship, however, mentors should periodically evaluate the extent to which it is productive and helpful to the protégé.

30
Carefully Consider the "Match"

A senior researcher at the National Institutes of Health, Dr. Kalb was known as a markedly influential scientist and a successful mentor to several generations of junior researchers in her field. Many of her protégés had gone on to attain eminence in the sciences. When asked about the "secret" to her success as a mentor, Dr. Kalb would smile and say "Simple. I only mentor a couple scientists at a time, and usually only those that remind me of myself. They are hardworking and intellectually curious researchers who would probably be very successful without my help. So, you might say I cheat and only mentor the great ones! It's really more than that though; I get to know all the new researchers but only mentor those I like, those who share my specific interests, and those who don't mind working as many long hours as I do."

Oil and water do not mix. Neither do some mentors and some protégés. It is a matter of chemistry. To increase the chances that your mentorships will flourish, spend time getting to know prospective protégés and try to figure out if you are compatible. A substantial body of research finds that mentors and protégés who are well matched on important personal and professional dimensions form stronger, more enduring, and more beneficial relationships. Good matching depends heavily on the context of mentoring and mentoring tasks. But personality traits (e.g., sense of humor, warmth, humility, extraversion), social skills, communication style, writing ability, personal values (e.g., importance of family versus work, religious commitment), short- and long-term career goals, and desired career trajectory also weigh in on the match.

A particularly salient cluster of matching variables between mentor and protégé includes work ethic, need for achievement, and "driveness." Mentors should ask themselves to what extent does a prospective protégé share their preference for structure, productivity, and rapid turnaround. Mentorships that are poorly matched in these areas are usually doomed to fail. Either the mentor will be frustrated by the protégé's lack of ambition or the protégé may find the mentor too complacent or relaxed.

According to studies on mentoring outcome, the more mentors and protégés consider themselves to be similar, the greater the perceived benefits of the mentorship. For obvious reasons, this finding is consistent with research on marriage. Although opposites occasionally attract, compatibility better predicts positive relationship outcomes. Some of the perceived benefits of well-matched mentorships are particularly worth noting; protégés from well-matched mentorships report receiving more social and career opportunities. Further, well-matched mentors and protégés are both more satisfied with and committed to the relationship.

Intentional consideration of a match assumes first an informal period of mentoring. Here the mentor and protégé have an opportunity to get to know each other due to their close working proximity. These arrangements often develop because the two parties work together without the pressure of a commitment to a formal relationship. Without the pressure, both parties are free to be themselves. It should be of interest to note that assigned mentorships are more superficial and less effective than unassigned mentorships. And it all relates to chemistry because personal commitment cannot be legislated. Consider arranged marriages. Sometimes they are successful, but seldom do they result in long-term satisfaction. Having a choice, like having a choice in marriage, yields the best outcomes in mentoring.

Equal access to a mentorship is another important consideration. Gender, race, age, ethnicity, and religion are often important matching concerns. However, these variables should not be used to limit protégés' opportunities for mentoring. Therefore, mentors should ascertain if they have biases that might interfere with their ability to effectively mentor someone who is different. Do they generally exclude members of certain groups? If so, why? Excellent mentors balance self-awareness and honesty regarding matching preferences with a willingness to ensure fairness and equal access in their selection of protégés.

Key Components

- *Choose protégés selectively from among those juniors you come to know informally.*
- *Consider important matching variables when choosing protégés.*
- *Remember that personality, communication style, personal values, and career interests are especially salient matching variables.*
- *Find protégés who share your level of ambition and drive.*
- *Balance matching concerns with efforts to ensure that potential protégés from underrepresented groups have a reasonable probability of becoming your protégé.*

31
Clarify Expectations

Alex, a new junior-level manager, immediately impressed David, a senior administrator in a large medical center. Alex was a quick learner, effective manager, and dedicated employee. After several months, David approached Alex about serving as his mentor—hoping to propel Alex expeditiously through the management pipeline. Although he came across as excited about this opportunity, Alex seldom scheduled meetings with David or took the initiative to meet informally. As a result, the two of them had very little interaction at first. David worried about this behavior. He decided to schedule a meeting and inquire about Alex's apparent avoidance. In this meeting, Alex admitted some apprehension about "wasting" David's time. He described a former supervisor who was easily angered by any intrusions. David realized he had neglected to clarify expectations about the mentorship and proceeded to do so. The two agreed to weekly "coffee breaks" and more formal monthly meetings. In addition, David clarified his expectation that Alex would "drop by" anytime he had a need to talk about a question, concern, or idea.

Everyone has expectations—expectations about life, work, and relationships. People have lofty hopes and dreams, anticipate advancements in their careers, and expect to have fulfilling lives. People carry expectations into relationships and mentorships are no exception. People may be aware of their expectations. But more than we might imagine, they are not consciously aware of what they expect. Yet expectations, whether or not people are aware of them, influence their behavior and interactions with other people.

Some people are astute enough to clarify their expectations and then to make them known. On the other hand, many people are not clear about their expectations, let alone making them known. In mentorships that prematurely terminate, researchers have found that misunderstanding and mismatched assumptions underlie mentorship dysfunction. During the formation stage of a mentorship, outstanding mentors initiate discussions of their expectations. They discuss a range of topics with their protégés. Among the important topics are the nature of the relationship, roles, responsibilities, frequency of contact, contexts for interaction, and a time frame for ending or decreasing contact. A critical aspect of the discussion is negotiation. Through a process of openness and give-and-take, mentors and their protégés should arrive at clear expectations that are mutually agreed upon.

One item to consider is both parties' previous experiences in mentorships. Previous experiences can exert a powerful influence on a new relationship, but the influence may go unnoticed unless it is openly talked about. Prominent psychologist Robert Sternberg wisely observed that each of us brings to relationships tremendously variable experiences, emotions, motives, and thoughts—our preconceived "story" of what a mentorship should be. This is our "ideal mentor story," and most of us have one. To establish an effective collaboration, mentors seek to understand the protégé's ideal story. Then they compare that story with their own ideal story. As conversations unfold, mentors and protégés should begin to see each others' point of view. This is when they negotiate, make concessions, and finally agree on mutually acceptable expectations.

The actual expectations sometimes are less important than the fact that they are discussed openly and made explicit. During the formation stage, for instance, frequency of contact is a critical issue. Protégés often want a lot of contact and detailed instructions. If the mentor is busy, such as one who travels frequently, this information must be clarified in advance, along with a clear plan for meeting when time allows. Other examples of clarifying expectations up front include specifying and negotiating expectations for things such as credit in shared projects, typical work style, and a mentor's relative strengths and weaknesses (e.g., the mentor is better at giving career advice and less comfortable with offering reassurance and counseling). These steps can prevent misunderstanding between the parties and eliminate unnecessary conflict.

The final item to remember is that mentors must take primary responsibility for clarifying expectations. Protégés are understandably novice. They do not have the knowledge and wisdom that mentors have gained through their professional experiences. In taking the initiative, mentors schedule the time needed to have a discussion about expectations. During the discussion, they relate to the protégé with considerable sensitivity. At this stage in their development, protégés may have significant self-doubts or hesitate to speak up because of the power differential in the relationship. To ensure that no stones are left unturned, mentors should revisit the issue of expectations from time to time.

Key Components

- *Explicitly discuss and clarify your expectations of protégés.*
- *Ask protégés to clarify their expectations for mentoring and for you as a mentor.*
- *Revisit expectations periodically, both to update them and to evaluate the extent to which they are being met.*
- *Be particularly careful to clarify expectations about frequency of contact, mentor roles, and protégé performance.*

32
Define Relationship Boundaries

When Greg, a partner in a consulting firm, and Caroline, one of several junior consultants in the firm, began a mentorship, both were concerned about the perceptions others might have of their relationship. They were determined not to let gossip or jealousies keep them from having a productive working relationship. Early in the relationship, they set boundaries. For instance, Greg recommended that they meet only at work and that they hold closed door meetings only when absolutely necessary. They also agreed not to socialize outside the firm. Finally, Greg asked Caroline's permission to include a second partner in all decisions regarding her salary and promotion. Greg explained that this safeguard would prevent his own feelings toward Caroline from unfairly disadvantaging other consultants in the firm.

Healthy mentorships are defined both by what they are and what they are not. Quite often, mentorships are defined by the mentor having multiple roles in relation to the protégé. Sometimes the many roles overlap. Mentors may serve as work supervisor, performance appraiser, advisor, project collaborator, and friend. In addition, mentorships often involve interaction in varied settings (office, off-site meetings, travel, and social gatherings). The overlapping roles and varying contexts for meeting do not need to result in inappropriate behavior or violations of personal boundaries. However, they do call for vigilance on the part of the mentor as mentorships are not defined as romantic or sexual partnerships. These types of relationships generally compromise the integrity of mentorships.

To avoid overstepping boundaries, mentors must define relationship boundaries and they should do so from the outset of the relationship. Here are important boundary issues to cover: (a) issues of confidentiality; (b) appropriate mediums or contexts for interaction; (c) frequency of contact; (d) acceptability of communication by phone (work and home) and email; (e) rules governing socializing; and (f) a strategy for handling uncomfortable dual roles such as collegial mentor and primary supervisor. The literature suggests that supervisory mentors, more so than non-supervisory mentors, must simply remain vigilant against potential harm they may inflict on protégés. The potential for harm is greatest when roles become confused or blurred.

Here is a helpful principle: The more roles added to a mentorship, the greater the risk for crossing boundaries. Here is another principle: The greater the risk for crossing boundaries, the more likely there will be negative outcomes in the mentorship. When mentoring is confined to developing a protégé in a work-related setting, risk of boundary violation is lowest. As the amount of time spent outside the traditional work setting increases and the list of reasons to interact grows, the risk of crossing boundaries also increases. Consider a mentor who becomes a business partner, religious director, psychotherapist, or best friend to a protégé. The potential for confusion and conflict escalates. The psychotherapist may discover evidence of emotional disturbance that reduces motivation to mentor or the best friend may be less able to deliver objective evaluation or needed confrontation. Although some mentors successfully play multiple roles, appreciation for the risks involved should not and cannot be easily dismissed.

No discussion of mentorship boundaries is complete without delving into romantic and sexual intimacies between mentors and protégés. Sexualized mentorships greatly increase the chance of harm while reducing the benefits to the protégé. When a mentorship takes on a sexual dimension, mentors compromise their ability to evaluate the protégé fairly and objectively. Protégés may feel trapped, fearing that their career advancement opportunities rest on yielding to the mentor's romantic or sexual overtures. Also, mentors unwittingly model exploitation and abuse of power. Substantial research shows that protégés who become sexually involved with mentors become more angry and regretful as time goes on. What is initially viewed as "mutual" by the protégé is often seen later as exploitive.

Key Components

- *Respect relationship boundaries between you and your protégé.*
- *Clarify appropriate contexts for interaction, any limits on confidentiality, and rules regarding socializing outside of the work setting.*
- *Avoid adding new roles (e.g., psychotherapy, business collaboration) to a mentorship.*
- *Refuse to allow a mentorship to become romantic or sexual.*

33
Consider Protégé Relationship Style

When the company human resources director asked Jeffrey to consider serving as a mentor in the new manager mentor program, Jeffrey agreed and looked for-

ward to a new challenge. His first protégé was Jim, a junior scientist from the re-
search and development department. At their first scheduled meeting, Jim was
courteous and responsive, yet somewhat uncomfortable as Jeffrey described the
typical course of mentorships in the program. During the next year, Jeffrey pro-
vided considerable information, teaching, and coaching as Jim began taking on
managerial duties. He noticed, however, that Jim became quite uncomfortable
when Jeffrey asked him how he was doing personally, tried to engage in small
talk, or generally showed an interest in him as a friend. It became obvious Jim
preferred only an "exchange of information," when the two met. Although Jef-
frey's mentoring appeared to help Jim understand and navigate company politics
and manager requirements, Jeffrey never got the sense that he really "knew" his
protégé. He eventually accepted Jim's stand-offish style and understood this as
Jim's broad approach to relationships. He continued to offer career mentoring
without expecting any reciprocal or friendly relationship to develop. When the
formal program ended, Jim seldom sought Jeffrey out and the two remained cor-
dial but formal in their connection.

Your mentorship is not the most important relationship your protégé will
ever have. Your protégé's most important relationship began long ago—at
birth actually. It may now be over, but its effects are pervasive. We refer, of
course, to your protégé's parental relationships. What were they like? Were
they reliable and loving? Did your protégé emerge secure and trusting or
disconnected and avoidant? Whatever your protégé's relationship style, remember this: although you had nothing to do with creating it, you had
better consider it carefully and tailor your approach to best fit this style.

Famed child development researcher John Bowlby was the first person
to demonstrate that children's interactions with their parents, typically
during the first year of life, have a profound impact on their interactions
with others throughout life. Bowlby's research shows that these early experiences influence the extent to which people seek out relationships, put
trust in other people, and develop their personality style. Not surprisingly,
he found that children who have a secure attachment base develop a sense
of trust and they are not anxious or insecure about undertaking new activities or forming new relationships as adults.

So what does attachment have to do with mentoring? As a mentor,
you likely will encounter protégés with one of three attachment or relationship styles. The style will dictate the nature of their receptivity to a

mentorship. *Secure* protégés have formed secure and trusting attachments to parents early in life. As protégés, they are likely to be more trusting and comfortable. Secure adults initiate and pursue mentorships more so than people from any other group. They have high self-esteem and are prone to assume that the motivations of others are benevolent. *Avoidant* protégés have not developed secure attachments to primary caregivers in childhood. Consequently, they do not easily trust others and generally spurn close relationships. Although a mentor can help an avoidant individual, it may be difficult to really describe the mentorship as a bonded relationship. *Preoccupied* protégés want closeness and relationship, but they remain unsure about whether they can really rely on others to come through for them. As protégés, they respond with ambivalence to mentoring. On the one hand, they enjoy a mentor's guidance and the care they receive. On the other hand, they fundamentally believe the mentor may prove unreliable. These protégés approach mentorship tentatively and they anticipate eventual disappointment with the relationship.

Which of these three relational styles characterizes your protégé? It is essential that you consider your protégé's style as one important facet of his or her personality. More than that though, it can dictate the very nature of your relationship. The secure protégé will be engaged and allow the mentorship to unfold in the direction of increasing closeness and collegiality. The preoccupied protégé may appear secure initially, but may occasionally withdraw or interpret minor oversights as evidence of mentor unreliability. The avoidant protégé is unlikely to enter into a mentorship in the first place, but in some organizations, may be assigned a formal mentor as part of a larger program.

The important thing is for mentors to reflect on these relational styles, adjust their expectations, and approach mentoring accordingly. Secure protégés can handle the texture and intensity of a healthy relationship. Avoidant protégés can appreciate various career mentoring functions but will be overwhelmed by and actively run away from all things personal or relational. Finally, the preoccupied protégé will require particular patience and consistency as he or she goes through periods of ambivalence and retraction from relational connection.

Key Components

- *Remember that protégés bring their own relationship style to the mentorship.*
- *Accept the fact that some protégés will be quite receptive to a relationship while others will be avoidant or ambivalent.*
- *Let the protégé's style guide your approach to mentoring.*
- *Recognize that secure protégés will benefit from career and relational functions while avoidant protégés will only accept career functions.*

34
Describe Potential Benefits and Risks

A famous author and popular professor, Oscar had been nominated for the Pulitzer for his writings in economics. Paradoxically, he was also considered a "thorn" in the University's side. His revolutionary ideas and bombastic style often caused him to be reviled and rejected by colleagues and administrators. Oscar occasionally agreed to mentor a younger "star" in his subspeciality in economics, but whenever he did, he was careful to offer what he called "informed consent." He warned faculty that association with him might "make your career, sink your career, or both!" Oscar elaborated that although he was successful in helping new professors get grants and gain international recognition, association with him also resulted in his protégés receiving occasional jibes and rejections from colleagues Oscar had alienated. He felt that prospective protégés should understand the assets as well as potential liabilities in committing to a mentorship with him.

Inherent in all mentorships are potential risks and benefits. Some of these consequences are not always apparent. Therefore, as much as possible, mentors should inform protégés about the primary risks and benefits associated with mentoring. In the majority of cases, mentorship outcomes are almost exclusively positive from the protégé's perspective. Salient benefits include more rapid professional development, greater satisfaction with training and one's career, faster promotion rates, larger salaries and total compensation packages, accelerated career mobility, and a stronger sense of competence and confidence in one's job. In short, protégés have more opportunities, are better compensated, and feel more prepared to succeed in their field. Because of these benefits, some professionals believe that identification with a mentor should be considered a major developmental task in one's early career.

Although the benefits usually outweigh the risks in mentor relationships, some risks do exist. Animosity or professional jealousy on the part of peers is a salient risk. The infamous "black halo" effect is another. Here the protégé's career is adversely affected when a mentor falls out of favor in the organization. Then there are the mentorships that turn sour. Here one or both parties feel disenchanted, disappointed, or emotionally wounded, which may occur for a variety of reasons such as unmet expectations, feelings of abandonment, or jealousy.

Mentors can take a couple of steps to help protégés in this area. First, they can discuss potential risks early in the relationship or even before the protégé commits to the mentorship. This shows respect by giving the protégé an informed choice. An informed protégé may decide that the potential risks are not worth the commitment. On the other hand, an informed protégé is better prepared to help prevent any negative outcomes or handle them if they occur.

Second, mentors can be open and honest about benefits and risks they stand to incur in the relationship. Mentors benefit by increasing their productivity, gaining recognition for their mentoring abilities, and experiencing satisfaction associated with seeing a talented junior professional thrive. Mentoring is often a good way to create a network of good colleagues and friends. Mentors may enjoy years of ongoing collaboration with protégés. Occasionally, successful protégés may even become sources of opportunity and advancement for the mentor.

On the down side, mentors risk guilt-by-association if the protégé fails or behaves inappropriately. They also risk loss of time and resources if a protégé drops out of a program or organization, does not advance, or fails to live up to expectations. These outcomes would make a mentorship a poor investment. By discussing these issues, protégés can gain a better appreciation of the reciprocal nature of mentorships. They also can gain a better understanding of their responsibility in the relationship. Of course, mentors cannot hold themselves responsible for knowing every possible risk and benefit. Just when you think you have seen it all, an unexpected risk or benefit might surface. The important thing is to be transparent and approach the discussion with an attitude of concern for the protégé.

Key Components

- *Be open and transparent about the benefits and risks of being a mentor.*
- *Discuss the likely benefits of mentoring for the protégé.*
- *Discuss the potential risks of mentoring for the protégé.*

35
Be Sensitive to Gender

Andrew was a sensitive and committed mentor. Nevertheless, he recognized from the start that his ability to mentor Amy in certain areas was limited by their gender differences. An excellent coach and teacher, Andrew helped Amy quickly learn the ropes in his area of consumer marketing. Although helpful and supportive, he suddenly found himself stumped. He was unsure how to respond to Amy's concerns about one day starting a family and balancing motherhood with her career. He was also surprised and unsure how to respond when Amy voiced concerns about "sexist" company policies. Andrew decided to openly discuss his concern about not having any first-hand experience relating to Amy's family concerns or concerns about company policies. But he did not rest there. He reaffirmed his unconditional support and asked her how he might go about helping her with gender-based policy issues. He also encouraged her to consider a secondary mentorship with a female manager.

When mentoring someone of the other gender, mentors have to consider how the differences might impact the mentorship. Admittedly, issues of gender may be important in same-sex relationships. But these issues are likely to have their greatest impact in cross-sex mentorships—especially when the mentor is male and the protégé is female. Why is this so important? Most mentors to women are men, and in many organizations or professional contexts (e.g., academia, engineering), senior professionals (prospective mentors) are more often male. A number of comprehensive research reviews show that women in cross-sex relationships benefit just as much as women in same-sex relationships and that mentored women reap greater tangible rewards (e.g., higher salaries, improved upward mobility) than their nonmentored peers. Because men historically enjoyed greater access to organizational resources and professional networks, they were able to offer women more substantial mentoring benefits. Of course, this should change as women continue to attain higher rank and status in most organizations.

Mentors should be sensitive to the many stressors and barriers women encounter (e.g., discrimination, stereotyping, social isolation, higher levels of marriage-work conflict, lack of access to information about networks, perceptions that women lack the leadership, drive, or tenacity to succeed). They should realize that many women prefer collegial and egalitarian mentorships. They also should realize that many modern-day women oppose hierarchical relationships and want to share power. For these reasons, women are often attracted to same-sex mentors who also serve as collegial role models.

Male protégés may also require special consideration. Typically men are more advantaged than women when it comes to access to both mentors and organizational resources. Yet men increasingly struggle with issues of balancing work and family. Socialized to be competitive and work-centered, many men define their identity by their career success. Mentors must often help male protégés discover the virtue of cooperation, and the significance of providing for their families emotionally, not just financially. When male protégés have a woman as a mentor, they sometimes report discomfort and concerns about the mentor's organizational power. They are so accustomed to hierarchical relationships that they find egalitarian or subordinate relationships with women to be disconcerting.

The most important finding from research on cross-sex mentorships is that there is great potential for both benefit and harm and that the key to success is open communication between mentor and protégé about gender differences—including anticipated concerns and how to handle such issues. Cross-sex mentorships may produce powerful synergy as mentor and protégé bring different but complimentary strengths and perspectives to the relationship and tasks at hand. Conversely, cross-sex mentorships present a number of sobering relational complexities and risks. Some of these complexities are the parties' assumption of stereotypical roles in relating to each other (e.g., male mentor is domineering and female protégé is passive and compliant), compromised role-modeling efficacy as gender cannot be integrated in the mentor's example, increased intimacy and sexual tension due to mutual liking and admiration—leading both to excitement and anxiety, the development of destructive and sexualized rumors within the organization, and resentment on the part of the protégé's peers, leaving the protégé isolated and scorned.

The key to successfully navigating cross-sex mentorships is openness and here the mentor must take the lead. When the male mentor is open, the female protégé is more likely to be open. The same is true if the mentor is female and the protégé is male. The area in which mentors should be most careful pertains to emotional and sexual attraction. Research in many professions reveals the existence of sexualized male mentor–female protégé relationships. Although these types of relationships are clearly in the minority, they exist in a consistent and steady pattern. Such compromised relationships often are harmful to protégés and corrosive for organizations. These relationships can also harm mentors who must live with the psychological aftermath of the compromise or at times the career and marital consequences if the compromise is exposed. Why is this pattern so consistent? One theory suggests that some men feel threatened by feelings of dependency in nonsexual, intimate relationships with women. To combat these feelings, men use sexual conquest to reduce discomfort and regain power. The necessity of boundary-setting around these issues is unrivaled. Mentors should monitor their own behavior, seek consultation when appropriate, and limit or redefine the mentorship to safeguard the protégé's best interests.

Key Components

- *Consider the effects of gender, particularly sex differences, on the mentorship.*
- *Discuss gender differences openly and ask your protégé how gender impacts his or her work experience.*
- *Recognize the risk of romantic/sexual feelings in cross-sex mentorships and take steps to avoid inappropriate behavior with protégés.*

36
Be Sensitive to Race and Ethnicity

When new Internal Medicine residents enter the training program annually, they are assigned a faculty proctor to serve as advisor, and if the relationship so develops, a mentor. Martha noticed that one of her new charges, Raphael, was Mexican American and spoke with a strong Spanish accent. During their first meeting, Martha noted their differences and asked Raphael how this pairing might work for him. Apparently relieved by this invitation to comment, Raphael disclosed some culturally rooted reluctance about having a female mentor. Surprised by Martha's lack of defensiveness and her genuine interest in his cultural experience, the two frequently discussed cultural issues and, to Raphael's surprise, developed a strong and helpful mentorship during the next four years.

When mentoring someone of another race, mentors have to consider how the difference might impact the mentorship. A number of pernicious and destructive myths abound regarding mentoring protégé's who are racial and ethnic minorities. These include: (a) a good mentor can easily mentor junior persons from any background—race is irrelevant; (b) minority group protégés can only be mentored by same-race mentors; (c) mentors should only mentor those with whom they share race or ethnicity. These oversimplifications are not supported by research. Race and ethnicity are often important matching variables. Protégés from minority groups tend to prefer mentors of their own race. Same-race mentorships are often perceived (by both mentor and protégé) as providing increased levels of both emotional/relational and task-focused/career benefits as well as increased identification and interpersonal comfort.

Same-race mentorships also can carry some risks. Many of the risks stem from the scrutiny and high visibility of minorities in predominantly white organizations. The poor performance of a protégé may be perceived as stemming from the incompetence of the mentor. The perception may linger whether or not it is grounded in reality. The difficulties of the mentor may be projected on to the protégé. The projection may linger even if it is not grounded in reality.

Like their counterparts, minority professionals should have the opportunity to benefit from mentoring and not be encumbered by unfair innuendos. Because junior professionals from minority groups often have limited opportunities for same-race mentorships, white mentors should establish as a priority the mentoring of protégés from diverse groups. Because minority professionals often face more challenges in placement and promotion than their white counterparts, white mentors should be sensitive to the special challenge these protégés face in their attempts to be successful.

Harvard Business School professor David Thomas suggests that effective mentoring to minorities includes the following: (a) creating challenging assignments; (b) putting them in high-trust positions—thus communicating that they are high performers; (c) providing crucial career advice; (d) sponsoring and recruiting them into new positions; and (e) protecting them by confronting critics—particularly when criticism includes racial undertones.

Addressing race early in the mentorship is usually preferable. It gives both parties permission to discuss touchy issues or tensions whenever they arise. But research indicates that it is most important that mentor and protégé prefer the same strategy for handling the issue of race. Two primary strategies have been identified for how people handle racial differences. These strategies are opposite of each other. In *direct engagement,* both parties openly discuss and process race issues. In *denial and suppression,* both parties avoid such processing. According to research findings, what matters most is an agreement between mentor and protégé on which strategy is used—not the strategy itself! We think there is a kernel of truth in this finding. However, we assert that it is in the best interest of the mentorship when mentors and protégés agree on *direct engagement.*

Outstanding mentors are aware of their own racial schemas and stereotypes. They look for opportunities to promote and encourage the careers of junior minority personnel. They directly broach the subject of race and ethnicity with minority group protégés, yet work to match their protégé's preferences for processing race issues. They recognize that minority group protégés may have unique mentoring needs and they work to better understand the experiences and preferences of their minority group protégés.

Key Components

- *Deliberately mentor junior minority professionals.*
- *Discuss racial differences openly throughout the mentorship.*
- *Work to understand the experience and unique mentoring needs of minority group protégés.*
- *Recognize that same-race minority mentorships may invite greater organizational scrutiny for both parties.*

37
Plan for Change at the Outset

During the first few months of their developing mentorship, Gail and Shannon had frequent interaction, a strong sense of "synergy" or creative excitement about various investigative writing projects, and a mutual sense that the relationship would be both productive and enjoyable. As a senior overseas correspondent for a major newspaper, Gail occasionally mentored well-matched junior journalists assigned to her foreign office headquarters. These mentorships were meaningful and career enhancing. But Gail had learned that the company generally rotated new journalists back to New York after three years. For this reason, Gail was careful to discuss this eventuality with Shannon and to clarify at the outset of the relationship that she expected the active phase of their mentorship to last no more than three years. The two discussed in advance how they would honor and celebrate Shannon's transition to new responsibilities, and if both agreed, how they would redefine their relationship and perhaps continue collaborating in some form.

From the beginning of the relationship, mentors should plan for the development, change, and eventual ending of the formal aspect of the mentorship. Early in the formation of a mentorship, both the mentor and protégé experience excitement, synergy, and some degree of mutual need fulfillment; both anticipate the benefits to come from the relationship. From this early vantage point, however, it may be difficult to soberly anticipate the changes necessary for maximal health and usefulness. By definition, mentorships are developmental relationships. If the protégé does not change, mature, and ultimately require less formal mentoring, something is drastically wrong. As in healthy parent-child relationships or marriages, good mentorships adapt to the changing circumstances and needs of the partners. Otherwise, they risk stagnation and disintegration.

As a benchmark, traditional mentorships in business and management settings endure for an average of five years. In actuality there is wide variation in the actual length of specific mentorships. Some terminate after several months of intense collaboration, while others last for decades after the most active phase of the mentorship has ended. Sometimes, it takes a death to end a mentorship. Regardless of their duration, many mentorships proceed through four predictable yet somewhat overlapping phases. The *initiation* phase typically is a period of 6–12 months. During this phase, the mentor and protégé get to know each other, begin working together, and commence a mentoring relationship. The *cultivation* phase typically lasts 2–5 years. Most of the active and intensive mentoring occurs during this phase and during this stage the mentor typically provides the widest range of mentor functions beginning with career functions (coaching, teaching, sponsoring) and also including psychosocial functions (support, encouragement, and friendship). During this phase, mentors and protégés must give up their idealizations—both of each other and of the mentorship. They have to accept the realistic limitations of mentorship, perhaps allowing their ideal views to give way to a good or adequate view of the relationship. The point is that they must let reality set in.

In the *separation* phase, the nature of the mentorship is substantially altered by structural changes in the organization (typically, one or both parties moves on) or by psychological and developmental changes within one or both individuals. At times, these changes are anticipated. At other times, these changes come about suddenly, catching either party or both parties off guard. Finally, if the mentorship does not end entirely during the separation phase, it will enter the final phase, known as *redefinition*. Here the mentorship evolves into an entirely new shape and form. The interaction is less intense and the parties experience more collegiality. We should note that, while these phases are useful guides, they are approximations and do not apply equally across mentorships.

Mentors should anticipate change at the outset and work with protégés to plan flexible time frames for the transitions and even termination of the mentorship. They should discuss the desirable milestones (e.g., graduation, promotion, assignment to a different division, or the protégé's sense of increased confidence and preference for increasing independence) that might signal to both the mentor and protégé that the relationship requires redefinition. They also should take the lead in narrating these changes as they occur (e.g., "you know, you're really becoming more independent. I'm impressed with your confidence. I notice that you don't need my advice so much these days—a sign you are mastering your work! Although I'll miss our close work together, I'm delighted to see you succeed and move ahead").

An inevitable consequence of redefinition and separation are some feelings of loss. And separation can be difficult for both the protégé and mentor, depending on the intensity of the relationship, their bonding, and their sense of fulfillment and achievement. The actual experience of loss, therefore, varies from mentorship to mentorship. The helpful and healthy action to take is to acknowledge up front the inevitability of separation, accepting that life is unpredictable, that the mentorship may endure in some form for a time, that it may end prematurely due to circumstances beyond either party's control, or that the mentorship has become unproductive or harmful.

Concerned mentors help protégés to work through their feelings of loss. It might be helpful for them to assist their protégés in moving through the stages of grief associated with relationship endings. A number of self-help resources are useful to this end.

In addition, mentors may need to work through their own feelings of loss. One of the most trying experiences of parenthood is separation and the subsequent empty nest syndrome. The child does not cease to exist, but may be moving on to a life of personal fulfillment. Still, there is loss, melancholy, and a sense of missing. In a similar vein, protégé development and separation can have a strong emotional impact on the mentor. The separation from a protégé may surface a full spectrum of emotions, including relief, joy, gratitude, and sadness. It is in the mentor's best interest to acknowledge these emotions and find ways to manage them constructively. Otherwise, the mentor may become overwhelmed and mishandle the separation.

Key Components

- *Understand that mentorships travel through predictable phases including initiation, cultivation, separation, and redefinition.*
- *Plan for and welcome growth in your protégé as well as transitions in the relationship.*
- *Discuss relationship changes as they occur and find ways to recognize and honor them.*
- *Accept the emotional side of mentorship separation and ending.*

38
Schedule Periodic Reviews
or Evaluations

A high school principal and prolific mentor, James typically had two or three "rising star" teachers whom he mentored. His protégés moved to leadership positions in the school, and ultimately, in the larger school district. Known for his personal organization and attention to detail, James kept files on his protégés for the purpose of documenting their career goals and tracking their progress. As soon as James determined that a mentorship was forming, he scheduled a formal meeting with the teacher, explained that he was willing to serve as a mentor to promote and support the person's career development, and inquired about their aspirations and ideal career trajectory. He then used this information to guide them toward relevant teaching experiences, appropriate graduate courses, and key committee assignments. Twice annually, he would meet with each of his protégés to monitor their career progress and evaluate the quality and value of the mentorship.

As the mentorship begins, the mentor should develop an intentional plan for review and evaluation. The most productive mentorships are those in which both parties actively participate in a systematic process of evaluation that aids in the protégé's professional development. Although this evaluation process need not be technical, laborious, or excessively formal, it will ensure that the relationship's health and productivity are episodically assessed. Mentors should take the lead in discussing the significance of periodic evaluations and then tentatively schedule appointments for the purpose of mutual review and evaluation of the mentorship. More frequent evaluation is often helpful early in the relationship (e.g., every 3–6 months), while more mature mentorships may require less frequent evaluation (e.g., annually or less often if the separation phase has already occurred). When the mentor emphasizes goal-setting and subsequent assessment, the protégé becomes more attuned to outcomes and more prone to intentionally consider ideal mentorship outcomes.

What should be reviewed or evaluated by mentor and protégé? Some salient questions to ask are: Is the mentorship meeting both participants' primary needs (e.g., encouragement, support, coaching, assistance with research, collegiality)? Is the protégé making progress toward both short- and long-term career goals? Are there sources of conflict, frustration, or stress in the mentorship, and how can these be addressed? Does either party feel that his or her main expectations or hopes for the mentorship are not materializing? Why or why not? What can be done to address this situation? Have circumstances, interests, or needs changed such that the mentorship must transition to a different form or begin the process of ending?

Periodic and planned discussions of a mentorship help to ensure that the relationship is maintained, transformed, or dissolved as needed. Planned reviews and evaluations, when initiated by the mentor, also serve as powerful models for the protégé. It shows responsible and committed professionalism as well as a personal commitment to serve the best interests of the protégé. It cannot be overemphasized that evaluations will only occur if the mentor makes them a priority. Discussing this at the outset, scheduling and following through with evaluative conversations, and making subsequent adjustments demonstrate ethical and responsible mentoring practice.

If you plan to mentor a number of protégés over a period of years, perhaps even over the course of a long career, we recommend broader evaluation of your mentoring efficacy. First, consider collecting some standard data from protégés at distinct junctures in their careers. For example, you might keep track of your protégés' jobs, their records of achievement in the field, their level of compensation, and their level of satisfaction with their career and with their mentorship experience. When aggregated across a number of protégés, such data will be useful to you and perhaps to the organization that employs you. It offers a record of mentoring outcomes. Depending upon the nature of the data you collect, it may additionally shed light on your particular strengths and weaknesses as a mentor—offering grist for the self-improvement mill.

Second, periodically ask protégés for their feedback during the formal mentorship. Mentors should solicit protégés' ideas on what is helpful and what is not. The important point is that the mentor takes the protégé seriously and remains open to the feedback. Obviously, a certain amount of discretion is necessary. Protégés often have insightful feedback to share with mentors. Protégés also may have perceptions that are inaccurate and suggestions that lack sound judgment. In general, protégés will not be put off by requests for feedback and assessment. To the contrary, they are likely to appreciate the mentor's interest in improving the mentorship.

Key Components

- *Develop a plan for periodic review and evaluation of your mentorship.*
- *Work with your protégé to determine career goals and mentorship expectations and ways to evaluate progress toward meeting each.*
- *Review the mentorship more frequently at the outset and less frequently as the mentorship matures.*
- *Use periodic evaluation to determine the direction mentoring should take.*
- *Consider a strategy for evaluating your mentoring outcomes across protégés and over time.*

Knowing Thyself
as a Mentor

Matters of Integrity

We live in a culture of ambition and competitive productivity, but few of us are truly "up-to-date" with our own psychological, emotional, and spiritual status. Excellent mentoring demands self-awareness. Outstanding mentors are self-reflective; they frequently take time to become reacquainted their own feelings, needs, wishes, and fears. The wise mentor understands the need for periodic reintroduction to the self. We call such self-awareness *mindfulness* and propose that mindfulness is a crucial ingredient of both effective and ethical functioning as a mentor.

Mindful mentors understand that they have imperfections, limitations, and weaknesses. They respect this side of their humanness in much the same way that they appreciate their talents, capacities, and strengths. They are honest about who they are as individuals, living by the maxim: Know thyself. Because they are nondefensive and accustomed to thinking about their areas of vulnerability as well as their gifts, mindful mentors approach mentoring openly and as a challenging adventure. These mentors use their self-awareness to successfully navigate powerful yet delicate relationships with protégés.

Mindful mentors are also *congruent*. How they see themselves is consistent with who they really are. They are not *incongruent* in the sense of allowing a gulf to exist between the "front" they present to protégés and the internal sense the self experiences. Not surprisingly, such disparity leads to shame, denial, and self-blindness. In contrast, congruent mentors easily articulate thoughtful awareness of their own limitations: "You know, I'm aware of feeling unable to help you in this area. I feel uncomfortable giving you advice about something I don't know enough about myself." Congruent mentors say, "I don't know" easily and without traces of shame or discomfort. Incongruent mentors, on the other hand, may attempt to feign knowledge.

In this section, we describe those elements of mentoring that pertain to knowing thyself—elements that require self-awareness and a realistic appreciation of the limits of one's competence. Mindful mentors actively consider the consequences of serving in the mentor role—both the benefits and the risks. They practice self-care and intentionally model personal and professional health. Not only do excellent mentors ensure their own competence in the mentor role, they are oriented toward holding themselves accountable for their behavior as a mentor. Because no legislative or monitoring body serves to hold those who mentor accountable, good mentors must be constantly self-governing. Mindful mentors are realistic and honest about the attraction they experience to some of their protégés and they soberly appreciate the substantial power they wield over those they mentor. Although mentors are often recipients of adulation and fawning praise from protégés, they must be practitioners of humility. Finally, excellent mentors are ever vigilant to avoid exploiting protégés. Of course, this requires acute awareness of one's own desires and motivations. Mindful mentors temper personal ambition with an orientation toward service and the protection of their protégés.

39
Consider the Consequences
of Being a Mentor

An outstanding mentor, Jennifer was personally responsible for developing many of the company's star female executives. During her tenure as a senior vice president, she had mentored many new female managers and had developed a reputation as the company's resident "star-maker." Although Jennifer had always been

drawn to mentoring because of the satisfaction she derived from seeing her pro-
tégés grow and succeed, she became increasingly aware that her success in the
mentor role also was beneficial for her own career. Not only did she receive strong
praise and recognition from the CEO, her achievements in mentoring had been
directly linked to several substantial bonuses over the years. Jennifer responded to
this self-awareness in two ways. First, she accepted her success in this arena while
refusing to allow external rewards to become her primary motivation for men-
toring. Second, she was open with protégés about the various ways in which she
benefited from being a mentor.

Mentoring is a responsibility not to be taken lightly. It entails many benefits but many risks as well. First, let us consider the benefits. Although the literature on mentoring highlights the rich benefits for protégés, mentors also stand to reap benefits. Tangible or *extrinsic* benefits may include reductions in workload, technical assistance, development of a loyal support base, recognition, financial rewards, and enhancement of one's own network. These benefits are not the primary motivators for many mentors. Many mentors savor the *intrinsic* benefits of mentoring. The most common intrinsic benefits are personal rejuvenation; excitement in working with a talented, energetic junior; and the satisfaction that comes from helping someone else succeed.

Second, let us consider the risks. Potentially, the most insidious cost is the expenditure of time and energy. Other potential costs are high-visibility protégé failures, sabotage or undermining by unscrupulous or disloyal protégés, and subtle innuendo or overt animosity from other professionals who are threatened or jealous. Sometimes mentoring has costly repercussions for the mentor's personal life. A deep mentoring bond can reverberate into the mentor's marriage, creating confusion, discord, or jealousy. The time and effort put into mentoring can impinge on a mentor's social life, or it can take away valuable time from other responsibilities. In some situations, a mentor may lose perspective and become an institutional bully—all in the name of protecting a protégé. This obviously will erode credibility and latter may be regretted. Then there is the finding that women and minority mentors tend to be closely scrutinized. It is as though they are placed under a microscope, making their problems and missteps visible for the world to see. But the close scrutiny is unfair.

Others in the organization may encounter equivalent difficulties, but these are not broadcast throughout the organization.

Mentors need to appreciate the benefits and risks inherent in mentoring. Therefore, they should examine their motivations for mentoring. Awareness is a robust indicator of health and maturity in the mentor role. Many mentors are altruistic in that they have a strong sense of responsibility for serving and helping others develop. Yet they can delight in the experience of synergistic collaboration and they may enjoy the accolades of peers and protégés regarding their mentoring acumen.

Other mentors have a disturbing underside. They may be motivated by power, control, or manipulation. They may regard protégés as objects to be used. They may be conflict avoiders or conflict producers. All of these tendencies may reflect their unresolved issues. For example, individuals with control issues simply may be acting out of a feeling of victimization or from a deep sense of powerlessness. These developmentally arrested and needy mentors are likely to be toxic for protégés—not just because of their problematic motivations for mentoring but also because of their lack of self-awareness.

Key Components

- *Recognize and accept the benefits of being a mentor including extrinsic and intrinsic benefits.*
- *Recognize and accept the costs of being a mentor including expenditures, potential for failure, and organizational scrutiny.*
- *Remain vigilant to consequences on one's relational life external to work.*
- *Increase awareness of your motivations to mentor—including self-serving motivations.*

40
Practice Self-Care

In his protégé Eric, Frank saw an earlier version of himself. A talented young researcher, Eric was a new addition to the university's biological research institute.

On several occasions, Frank discovered that Eric had been in the lab all weekend or overnight. He cautioned Eric about overworking himself and neglecting his wife and infant child. Frank disclosed his own struggles with overwork and family neglect at times during his career and how this behavior had hurt more than it helped in the long run. More important, Frank shared how he learned to maintain clear boundaries (e.g., he went home at 5:00 P.M. each day regardless of how much work remained and he refused to take on new projects when he determined that doing so would outstrip his staff's time and resources). Frank also spent each lunch hour jogging and always invited new staff to find some time during the day in which they would exercise. Over time, Eric came to appreciate his mentor's emphasis on self-care and integrated many of these habits into his own approach to life and work.

Mentors who fail to care for themselves may reach a point where they are unable to care for their protégés. Eager to succeed, some mentors mistakenly disregard their own needs. But not even the greatest of mentors is superman or superwoman—just a capable human being. That is why mentors who endure over the long haul attend to their personal needs and consistently practice self-care. Let's face the facts: Mentoring is hard work. It requires time and resources beyond the normal work week. Mentors who fail to safe guard their physical and emotional health are setting themselves up to be of no benefit to themselves or their protégés.

On this subject, the research is clear about what protégés want from mentors. They want exemplars who can serve as a model of how to balance their professional and personal lives. They want to see in action—not just in theory—how to set boundaries. In the back of the mind of every protégé is a nagging question: "Can I have a successful career and still have a satisfying personal life?" The protégé looks at the lifestyle of the mentor for an answer.

Perhaps in the area of self-care, more than in any other area, it is paramount that mentors "walk the talk" and not simply "talk the talk." Preaching health and self-care but working excessively, neglecting one's physical needs, or failing to nurture important personal relationships only broadcast hypocrisy to protégés. Although some protégés will reject the mentor's lifestyle, others unfortunately will follow the mentor's example. The pattern of self-neglect then passes from one generation to the next.

How then do mentors practice self-care? They say "no" to new responsibilities or "opportunities" that compromise their health or quality of work. They follow through with commitments to family, friends, and protégés, and safeguard these relationships. As we said previously, they clarify their expectations and set boundaries with their protégés. In times of unusual need or high demand, mentors may make special requests to protégés or other colleagues (e.g., "I really need you to take more leadership on this new project," or "It would help me if I could honestly share with you my concerns about the organization, but I would need you to keep that information confidential," or "I'm feeling overwhelmed and burned-out lately. I'm going to take a few days off this week to rest and care for myself"). In all the cases cited above, mentors who make such requests avoid behaving as though they have no limits.

Key Components

- *Care for protégés by first caring for yourself.*
- *Understand that protégés need a mentor who models a responsible balance between personal and professional life.*
- *Just say "no" to excessive demands at work.*
- *Follow through with commitments to family, friends, and protégés*
- *Model self-care overtly by taking time off and limiting time devoted to work.*

41
Be Productive

Felicia's arrival as the newest faculty member in the university's history department was greeted with delight by many of the department's majors and graduate students. The students had grown weary of the department's reputation as a bastion of dead wood. This was a reference to the fact that most of this large department's tenured faculty members were not very productive. A couple of them occasionally published book reviews in second- or third-tier journals or they sometimes made presentations at professional meetings. But for the most part, the faculty's research and scholarly activity was not exciting. As a result, applications from prospective doctoral students had dropped to all-time lows. Things changed quickly when Felicia arrived and immediately formed a historical research group among the students. This weekly group generated a great deal of student interest and quickly became a sort of mentoring team. Not only did Felicia share drafts of her most recent articles and chapters of a forthcoming book, she organized several joint projects with students and submitted these for presentations at conferences. In addition to her active scholarly writing, Felicia modeled professional engagement as vice president of a national historical society and associate editor of a major journal in the discipline. Felicia's productivity was infectious. Within a couple of years, the number of graduate applications spiked. Many of the applicants specified an interest in working directly with Felicia.

You can only lead a protégé where you yourself have traveled. And you will be a more effective guide when you have traveled there recently. Of course, the best mentors are frequent flyers. Effective mentors are engaged in the professional landscape they claim as their own. They are deeply involved in the work of their discipline and are frequently in contact with colleagues and collaborators. Outstanding mentors assume leadership roles in the field and are seen by peers as hard workers and innovators. Whether their product is new business, innovative ideas, journal articles, or research findings, effective mentors simply produce.

There are many reasons why protégés are drawn to productive mentors. Productive mentors create excitement and possibility. They are enthusiastic, committed, and engaged. They trail a wake of innovative ideas, new projects, and career opportunities for protégés. Mentors on the cutting-edge in any field create visibility and strategic access to resources and influence for protégés. In university settings, the most productive scholars bring substantial grant funding to their institutions—including full financial support for protégés. They also bring visibility and prestige to their institutions. In business, productive leaders are rewarded with more resources and enjoy greater allocation of perks. In addition, productive mentors are ultimately the best models. Because they are actively involved in the work of the profession, they offer a tangible example of how to carry out complex professional tasks. If a mentor is not active in the job of focus, his or her effectiveness dissipates.

What about the unproductive professional? Lack of production in one's field is a red flag. Potential protégés may be advised to avoid this mentor altogether. Lack of productivity may signal one of three problems: (a) professional disengagement, (b) poor motivation, or (c) poor professional self-esteem. The disengaged mentor has become bitter or disenchanted with the profession. The unmotivated mentor sees no value in continuing to contribute or produce products in his or her field. The mentor with poor self-esteem feels insecure or unworthy—perhaps viewing oneself as incompetent and fearful of being revealed. Whatever the cause, unproductive people probably should not mentor. They cannot lead protégés where they have not traveled. Active and engaged productiveness is one hallmark of an ideal career mentor.

Key Components

- *Be active in your field and productive as a professional.*
- *Remember that your protégé will benefit both directly and vicariously when you model engagement and leadership in your profession.*
- *Evaluate reasons for drops in your productivity and consider whether you are the best mentor for a potential protégé.*

42
Make Sure You Are Competent

A newly minted PhD and a first-year professor in a large political science graduate program, Dr. Franklin was a solid teacher and researcher. He was competent in the subject matter in his courses and had a mature grasp of the academic/professional landscape his graduate students would soon be facing. Although adept in many regards, Dr. Franklin was less comfortable interpersonally. Shy and introverted by nature, he was typically reticent and awkward in interpersonal situations—including informal exchanges with students. Aware that mentoring required more than technical knowledge, Dr. Franklin began working with a psychologist at the university counseling center who was skilled in executive coaching. After a few months of intensive interpersonal skill development, he felt considerably more comfortable in structuring and managing relationships with students. Finally, in order to help safe-guard his students while improving his interpersonal acumen, Dr. Franklin asked a senior professor in the department for occasional supervision (discussion and advice) related to his various faculty–student mentorships.

Incompetence guarantees the lack of success. But to be successful, mentors really need two types of competence. They need to be competent in their professions and they need to be competent as mentors. Because there are no credential-checking agencies or professional organizations that certify mentoring competence; it is incumbent then upon mentors to ensure their own competence and fitness to mentor.

Mentor competence is rarely considered during a professional's training; let alone is it evaluated. This holds true in business and in academic settings. Holding positional authority or supervisory status in an organization is often equated with competence to lead, supervise, and mentor. We know this is not always true. Some people who try their hand at mentoring lack the technical or relational capabilities required for success.

Prospective mentors should honestly consider whether they possess the requisite on-the-job experience, professional expertise, wisdom, and knowledge to truly be of benefit to a prospective protégé. Because ethical guidelines in most fields prohibit professionals from practicing outside their area of competence or expertise, prospective mentors must engage in some self-analysis regarding competence or preparedness to effectively help another in a long-term developmental relationship. Mentors who are unsure of their own job performance experience *role ambiguity*. They are likely to receive lower motivation and performance ratings from protégés. Competent mentors must be experienced on the job at hand, confident and successful in their own right, and capable of safely and benignly managing relationships with protégés who remain largely vulnerable to the mentor's power throughout the course of the relationship.

Although some supervisors are technically competent mentors—imbued with the requisite experience, professional confidence, and ethical-mindedness—they are inept in managing relationships. Competence to mentor demands that mentors exudes benign personality characteristics as well as a good measure of interpersonal savvy. Listening skills, warmth, caring, and preferably a sense of humor, are needed. Without relational expertise, even the most technically competent mentor will find it difficult to effectively deliver career guidance. The seeds of coaching, teaching and guidance will wither if sewn upon parched interpersonal soil.

A word about technical competence: Real mentoring competence is made up of more than the sum many mentoring techniques. Although competence demands several focal skills (e.g., listening, challenging, encouraging), it is essential that the mentor also develop a knack or sense for knowing when to apply these in specific contexts with specific protégés for maximal effect. The competent mentor is able to discern when a protégé requires teaching and when to pause and simply offer emotional support. The competent mentor understands when a protégé requires collegial friendship and when direct confrontation will stimulate necessary growth. The bottom line is that competence is complex. It represents a rich and sometimes hard-earned mixture of natural aptitude, training, and experience in the mentor role.

Key Components

- *Work at developing your technical and relational mentoring skills.*
- *Evaluate your own experience, expertise, and confidence level before serving as a mentor.*
- *Understand that competent mentoring is more than the sum of its parts. Accurately select and deliver specific mentoring skills at important junctures to benefit your protégé.*

43
Hold Yourself Accountable

A seasoned supervisor in a large federal agency, George was well versed in the art of mentoring. As a mentor, he was skilled, dependable, and helpful to the junior managers he identified as most promising. His relationship with Tammy was typical of his approach to mentoring. Once George had identified Tammy as an especially excellent performer, and well matched with George's own interests and personality, he committed to helping her career. George set aside time for Tammy, always followed through when he promised to review her work or observe her in a meeting, and most important, he always gave her very kind but direct and honest feedback. As a result, Tammy never doubted George's integrity or reliability. Unknown to Tammy, George also met every month or so with a good colleague in another agency to engage in peer supervision and support. In this context, George shared concerns and solicited advice about how to best serve his protégés.

All enduring relationships are based on trust. Trust is the fabric or glue that binds mentor and protégé together in a safe, productive, and committed relationship. Stemming from the German word *trost*, meaning comfort, trust signifies a state of confidence and comfort in relation to a significant other. When a mentor's behavior is characterized by consistency, honesty, and integrity, trust can be established and maintained. The consistency applies to overt and covert forms of behavior.

Ensuring integrity and building trust happens when mentors intentionally hold themselves accountable. The accountability should occur on two levels—one with the protégé and one with at least one trusted colleague. Accountability with one's protégés involves a range of attitudes and commitments including doing no harm, placing the protégé's developmental needs first, and honoring commitments—from the smallest (diligence in keeping appointments) to the largest (protecting protégés even at substantial personal cost). Accountability also entails certain behaviors including clear communication, maintenance of confidentiality, setting and maintaining boundaries between personal and professional roles, and the delivery of honest and timely feedback—even when unpleasant.

Mentor accountability is incomplete without attention to maintaining at least one solid collegial relationship characterized by mutual self-disclosure surrounding one's mentorships. Within the safe scrutiny of a confidential peer relationship, a mentor can share any number of concerns. A mentor may discuss issues of competence, feelings about protégés, concerns about romantic attraction, blurring of professional and personal roles, and anything else that might arise in the context of mentoring. In long-term, complex, and emotionally intimate mentorships, mentors may occasionally experience anger, distress, self-doubt, guilt, and intense sexual or romantic attraction. When such thoughts and feelings are aired in the presence of a trusted and capable peer or superior, mentors are able to regain perspective and resolve the problem.

What about the erosion of trust in a mentorship? There are infinite ways of losing a protégé's trust, but they generally fall into two categories. *Overt* or "red letter" offenses easily erode trust. An example of an overt offense is when a mentor violates a protégé's confidence, steals a protégé's work, or becomes vindictive or exploitive. *Covert* violations of trust can be more insidious, emotionally confusing, and destructive to protégés than overt offenses. The subtle nature of these offenses makes them more difficult to identify, but their destructive consequences can loom large. Take the mentor who offers only marginal assistance in return for substantial protégé output or a mentor is who is covertly seductive. In both of these instances, the protégé is undermined but has to second guess the intentions of the mentor. In sum, be aware that protégé trust is hard to earn, easy to squander, and an utter necessity for effective mentoring.

Key Components

- *Ensure that your behavior is characterized by honesty, consistency, and integrity.*
- *Be accountable to protégés by honoring commitments.*
- *Be accountable to protégés by routinely conferring with at least one trusted colleague about your mentoring and your relationships with your protégés.*
- *Avoid endangering protégé trust through dishonesty, incongruence, or exploitation.*

44
Respect the Power of Attraction

Angie began mentoring Steve during his first year of study in an internationally known music conservatory. A gifted and energetic young pianist, Steve was a delight to teach and coach. Steve was clearly enamored and awed by Angie, a rather famous pianist, and Angie found that she enjoyed Steve's devotion and fawning attention. Angie found Steve to be bright, talented, and quite attractive. She

found collaborating with him interesting, exciting, and in some way, renewing.
As the year unfolded, Angie became increasingly aware of powerful feelings of at-
traction toward Steve. Angie's marriage worsened as she spent an increasing
amount of time fantasizing about a romantic future with Steve. Finally, aware
that she was losing the ability to objectively and helpfully evaluate Steve's
progress, Angie sought out a colleague in the conservatory and shared her feelings
about Steve. After some good consultation, she agreed it best to transition Steve
to another faculty pianist. Although she accepted her human feelings of attrac-
tion, and saw them as a not uncommon facet of a close cross-gender mentorship,
she simultaneously recognized the power differential in the relationship, the eth-
ical difficulties involved in embarking on a relationship with a trainee, and the
obvious risk to Steve of feeling coerced or exploited by his mentor. She remained
supportive of Steve's career but limited her contact with him.

In close working relationships, developing interests that go beyond work is not uncommon. Attraction is a powerful force and only naïve professionals deny this reality. Mentors sometimes experience intellectual, emotional, romantic, and sexual attraction to their protégés. Attraction often involves some combination of these features. But attraction itself is not a problem. It is human. Denial of attraction and the mishandling of attraction are the real problems. These responses get mentors into trouble.

Problems associated with attraction are most common in mentorships in which the mentor is male and the protégé is female. This is partially a result of the large proportion of men at senior levels in many organizations and partially a function of deeply entrenched attitudes of men about sexualizing relationships with women. Considering that mentorships are formed on the basis of shared interests and some degree of compatibility and that the relationship may extend over a long period of time, it is not surprising that the cross-gender mentorship context is ripe for developing intimacy.

Problems of attraction also may occur in same-gender mentorships. The problems can range from strong sexual interests to codependency. The attraction may go either way—from mentor to protégé or from protégé to mentor. The attraction may also be reciprocal—both individuals are attracted to each other. Usually the attraction comes as a surprise. Nevertheless, it must be dealt with by the mentor in a responsible manner.

Few mentors receive training to help them handle attraction in professional relationships. This is despite the fact that many protégés, especially women, report sexual contact with educators and supervisors. Even when there is no physical involvement, mentors may experience feelings of guilt, shame, anxiety, and confusion due to their emotional involvement. The worst cases are when mentors become physically involved but delude themselves that the relationship is merely collegial. They ignore the mentor–protégé power differential and fail to anticipate the long-term consequences of their involvement.

How then should mentors respond to the power of attraction? First, develop self-awareness. They should ask themselves these questions: "How often am I thinking about this person and in what way?" "Do I treat this protégé preferentially?" "What are my fantasies about where this relationship may be headed?" "What emotional needs am I trying to get met in this mentorship?" Second, accept your humanness. Mentors can engage in constructive self-talk such as "It makes good sense that I find this person attractive, we are well-matched in many areas, and he or she is quite talented. Thank goodness I am human and can experience attraction. It is not a catastrophe." Third, get consultation. We mean the collegial accountability referred to in element 43. Discuss the attraction and its roots and devise a plan for responding. Of course, discussing such attraction with the protégé is often not necessary and carries the risk of merely heightening the experience or introducing turmoil for the protégé. In some mentorships, those that are well-developed and characterized by a great deal of maturity on the part of both members, attraction can be discussed at various times as a way of ensuring accountability to professional boundaries. In most cases, however, it is the mentor's responsibility to carefully attend to evidence of growing attraction, consult with a colleague, and devise a plan either for continued mentoring, or in a few cases, termination of a mentorship that can no longer be professionally productive.

Can a mentorship ever become a deeper relationship without harming the protégé? In some circumstances, yes. Examples exist in business, academia, and other settings of the mentor–protégé pair who become apparently well-adjusted and happily married spouses. A problem with these exceptional cases is that they serve to distract from the vast majority of romanticized and sexualized mentorships that do not end happily. In most cases the protégé feels exploited and simultaneously deprived of a long-term mentor.

Another problem is that these types of relationships violate ethical codes in some professions. For example, dual relationships are unethical for psychologists. The ethical principle rests on the premise that psychologists can compromise the quality of their service delivery. Therefore, a clinical supervisor who has sexual intimacies with a psychology intern may not be able to provide an impartial evaluation of the intern's performance. Impairment in the supervisor's judgment can have negative consequences for the intern not only personally but also professionally.

Key Components

- *Accept attraction as a common and expected phenomenon in well-matched mentorships.*
- *Maintain self-awareness regarding feelings of attraction toward protégés.*
- *Seek out collegial consultation when attraction threatens to undermine or negatively alter professional boundaries.*
- *In most cases, do not disclose attraction to protégés.*
- *Remember that romantic involvement with a protégé constitutes a breach of professional boundaries and will probably not help the protégé.*

45
Accept the Burden of Power

When Peter reflected on his career as a faculty member of a medical residency and mentor to several generations of surgery residents, he often smiled and shook his head at some of his early career blunders. As a young and experientially green supervisor, Peter had often failed to appreciate the profound power he wielded vis-à-vis his residents. During those early years, Peter frequently blurred boundaries with residents (e.g., socializing, dating, developing close personal friendships) and tended to minimize the impact of his positional authority. In order to feel like "one of the gang," Peter minimized his role as supervisor and evaluator—often causing confusion among his residents. As Peter matured, he developed an increasingly sober appreciation for the tangible power he held in relation to those

he supervised. His evaluations carried real weight in influencing a resident's
ranking and subsequent job possibilities. Peter gradually realized that his denial
of power actually undermined his credibility with residents. He became careful
about boundaries with students and conscientious in the use of his positional
power for the benefit of those he mentored.

Power is influence. In all mentorships, there is an implicit power differential between the mentor and protégé. The mentor is in the one-up position, while the protégé is in the one-down position. Mentors can use their position of power for good or they can abuse their power.

Wise mentors acknowledge that they wield substantial power. Seasoned and successful members of any organization or profession are the most influential and potent developers of junior personnel. This is the mentor's *reflective power*. The credibility, resources, and reputation of the mentor extend to the protégé; the protégé receives early credibility and entrée into important arenas of an organization precisely because he or she is associated with a powerful sponsor. Mentoring, by its very definition, signifies an unequal helping relationship focused primarily on the development of the protégé. This inherent power inequality makes mentoring a fiduciary relationship—a professional relationship in which partners are not on equal terms. The fiduciary party (mentor) must act with utmost good faith and solely for the benefit of the dependent party (the protégé).

The mentor's power emanates from several sources. First, mentors often hold supervisory/evaluative authority over the protégé. Mentors may be key contributors to decisions about the protégé's ultimate success or failure. A mentor's endorsement will exert tremendous influence on whether the protégé will be competitive for subsequent jobs and promotions. Second, mentors are subject matter experts; they wield the power of authoritative knowledge, experience, and wisdom. Finally, mentors hold the emotional power of affirmation or endorsement that the protégé indeed belongs in a profession. Although many protégés may discount the significance of this parental form of power, it often has a deep impact on personal/emotional levels and contributes significantly to one's sense of belonging. The mentor's endorsement serves as an antidote to the imposter syndrome commonly experienced by neophyte protégés.

Some mentors misunderstand, underestimate, disregard, or have difficulty in accepting the power inherent in their role. Younger supervisors and those newest to their profession often have difficulty accepting the mantle of authority. Like the rebellious prince who refuses to assume duties as king, so the new mentor may work to deny or repress evidence of relative power vis-à-vis his protégés. Feeling insecure or fearful of possessing positional authority, this mentor hides from power and seeks inappropriate peership with protégés. These actions compromise mentoring and confuse protégés. When parents or teachers shirk authority and attempt to join in with children, healthy kids rebel or reject them. When a mentor refuses to accept power and use authority constructively, the power of their position is inadvertently diminished.

When mentors accept the burden of power and honor the power differential between themselves and their protégés, they significantly reduce the probability of exploitation and harm emanating from the abuse of power. Mentors abuse power when they withhold resources or opportunities based on irrelevant criteria. They abuse power when they place their own needs ahead of the needs of their protégés. Coercing emotional, sexual, or career favors from protégés and giving them no options but compliance or reprisal illustrates such abuse. At times, the coercion is direct and overt. At other times, however, coercive power is subtle. A mentor may discredit any idea a protégé puts forth when the real goal is to get the protégé to accept the mentor's view. A mentor may require adulation and attention from protégés. This is often an act of manipulation because the protégé faces the possibility of falling out of the mentor's good graces. Another abuse occurs when mentors fail to use their power to help protégés, especially when they are in the position or have the ability to do so. The failure to use power constructively can be as abusive as direct coercion.

Key Components

- *Accept the power you hold relative to your protégé.*
- *Recognize that your protégé benefits from your organizational power and credibility.*
- *Respect the power differential in the mentorship.*

- *Act solely for the benefit of your protégé.*
- *Use power to encourage, support, and bolster, but never to exploit.*

46
Practice Humility

In nearly every way, General Frank Hastings was a model Marine Corps officer. A Naval Academy graduate, a combat veteran, and a very articulate and effective leader, General Hastings was well-loved and well-respected by congressional leaders, peers, and subordinates. One of those subordinates, Major Greene, was General Hastings's aide and his primary protégé. One of the things that most amazed Major Greene about his mentor was the general's profound and apparently authentic humility and humanness. Although the general was very success-ful, he seemed to go out of his way to highlight his shortcomings, tell others about his mistakes, and laugh about his fallibility. Paradoxically, this habit further en-deared the general to those around him. For example, whenever the major referred to the general's combat exploits or career successes, General Hastings would look him in the eye and say something like "Major, I was in the right place at the right time. I'm a lucky man, and fortunate enough to be surrounded by brave and smart people—people like you." Although the general admitted that he was good at cer-tain tasks and refused to engage in false displays of humility, he reveled in both ac-cepting his limitations and modeling this acceptance to protégés.

Mentors who are self-aware, nondefensive, open to feedback, and humble in their self-assessments are highly preferred by protégés. One interesting line of mentoring research shows that mentors who underestimate the ef-fectiveness of their leadership receive the highest quality-of-mentoring ratings from protégés. Some level of sober, critical self-evaluation appears to be a prerequisite for outstanding role modeling. Transformational men-tors are humble, modest, and conservative in their self-assessments. The humble mentor is perceived as approachable and real. In owning and even highlighting blemishes and imperfections, the mentor offers the protégé some real texture. "Perfect" mentors, or more accurately, those who feign perfection, are distant, untouchable, and therefore, unlikely to receive the protégé's reciprocal confessions of anxiety and struggle.

A defining feature of humility is an appreciation of one's limitations. The more accurate people are in their self-assessments the more this is a reflection of humility. Humble people are not afraid to take an honest look at themselves—warts and all.

Effective mentors readily admit, "I don't know" when this is true and are comfortable (versus enraged or mortified) when protégés see the limits of the mentor's expertise. They are not arrogant, self-absorbed, or narcissistic but reasonably self-confident and professionally poised. As we have already pointed out, excellent mentors are highly accomplished and competent. So there is no contradiction between humility and competence. The key is that the humble mentor appreciates his or her assets as special gifts not as evidence of personal grandeur. Mentors of this ilk focus less on self-centered outcomes and more on the developmental needs of protégés.

A humble mentor can model humanness and imperfection without shame or distress. Because he or she does not demand adulation from subordinates, the humble mentor is more available for mutuality and collegiality—the benefits of a real relationship. When humility is absent, the relationship is superficial and characterized by grandiose unreality. Further, the mentor may be intolerant of a protégé who elects a career path that diverges from that followed by the mentor. Finally, the mentor may be threatened and subsequently disparaging and rejecting of the protégé who is not satisfied to be cloned in the image of the mentor.

Key Components

- *Practice humility through nondefensiveness and transparency with respect to faults and weaknesses.*
- *Understand that by authentically admitting limitations, you give your protégé permission to be human as well.*
- *Acclimate yourself to the idea of admitting mistakes and saying "I don't know."*
- *Appreciate your own strengths and accomplishments while using them to promote your protégé, not gratify yourself.*

47
Never Exploit Protégés

*As principal at a large suburban middle school, Don supervised a primarily fe-
male teaching staff. Although known as an exceptional leader and career-helper,
there had been a few problems in Don's mentorships over the course of his career.
On three occasions, female protégés had either abruptly discontinued a previously
close and productive mentorship or had transferred to other schools. When queried
about the reason for their sudden withdrawal, these women gave somewhat
vague suggestions that the relationship had become "too intense" or "too stressful."
After the third incident, Don stopped and began to take stock of his mentoring
style. He recognized a pattern on strong emotional dependence on his protégés. A
divorced and lonely man, Don depended on his female protégés routinely to meet
his needs for companionship and affirmation. Although he was never sexually
harassing or exploitive, Don's neediness proved to be overwhelming and alien-
ating to the women he was otherwise quite adept at helping.*

Exploitation is the selfish use of someone else for one's own ends or
profit. It translates into treating people as objects rather than as human
beings. Exploitation also involves taking an unfair advantage. A person in
a position of relative power and authority exploits a person who is in a
power-down, dependent, or vulnerable position. Although most mentors
are repelled by the notion of exploiting a protégé and thereby sullying an
inherently trusting and benevolent relationship, evidence suggests that
protégés are frequently exploited in a variety of ways.

Surveys of graduate students and junior managers find an alarming
number of women who report sexual harassment or sexual contact with
male mentors. As time elapses from the actual occurrence of these experiences, these protégés report feeling increasingly exploited and negatively
impacted. Although mentors (male or female) often experience protégés
as mature colleagues, conscientious mentors acknowledge to themselves
their ever-looming potential to be exploitative.

Sexual exploitation unmistakably is a "bright-line" offense that most
mentors clearly recognize and guard against. But other forms of exploitation exist as well. Some are more subtle than sexual exploitation. How-

ever, these too can have harmful consequences. The most common of these include emotional and professional exploitation. Emotional exploitation occurs when the mentor (often unaware) attempts to use the mentorship—and the protégé—to satisfy unmet and often powerful emotional needs. Requiring the protégé to listen at length to personal complaints and dissatisfactions or demanding adulation and fawning allegiance from protégés can be exploitive. Professional exploitation may occur when a mentor takes unfair advantage of the protégé's work or professional products. When a manager or professor presents a protégé's work as entirely (or even primarily) his or her own, the mentor is exploiting the protégé. In other cases, a mentor may demand exceptional productivity and devotion to long work hours on the part of a protégé without ever legitimizing the mentorship through comparable coaching, sponsorship, or support. This relationship is exploitive simply because it benefits the mentor exclusively.

Subtle forms of exploitation are not always easy to detect. However, they are usually preventable. What mentors must keep at the forefront of their thinking is how their protégés benefit from the expectations, assignments, and demands placed on them. If benefits can be identified, more than likely, the chances of exploitation are reduced. If benefits to the protégé cannot be identified, the chances of exploitation are greatly increased. An important question for mentors to ask themselves is this: "How do I benefit from this expectation versus how does my protégé benefit?" By intentionally keeping the focus of the mentorship on the protégé's growth and development and by accepting their inherent power in relation to protégés, mentors reduce the probability that a mentorship will become exploitive.

Key Components

- *Avoid taking unfair advantage of protégés.*
- *Recognize that protégés are usually vulnerable to some extent to exploitation.*
- *Be aware of both overt (e.g., sexual) and subtle (e.g., emotional, professional) temptations to exploit.*

When Things Go Wrong

Matters of Restoration

Mentorships are special relationships. Nothing compares to the dynamics that exist between a mentor and protégé. But mentorships are similar to other relationships in one important respect: They are imperfect and subject to human foibles. Some mentorships become riddled by conflict, dissatisfaction, or result in disturbing endings. Some become unhealthy, dysfunctional, and even emotionally or physically destructive. This is the dark side of mentoring that some mentors do not always want to face.

Mentors should be open to the possibility that things can go wrong. Because of their inherent imperfections and those of their protégés, mentors need to be alert to situations and interactions that might undermine their relationships. If things go wrong, they must address the problems quickly and attempt to restore the relationship.

How do mentors know when their relationships are in trouble? Among the many warning signs, three stand out as prominent.

- The protégé or mentor does not believe some of their important developmental or professional needs are being met.
- The protégé or mentor senses that the costs of the relationship outweigh the benefits.
- The protégé or mentor feels distressed or harmed by the relationship.

A substantial body of research shows that when protégés and mentors feel disenchanted, upset, or that they have been harmed in mentorships, they often report some casual problems or events. Specific causes include poor matching between mentor and protégé (i.e., dissimilar backgrounds, interests, personality style), faulty communication, incongruent expectations, role conflicts (i.e., evaluative/supervisory versus helping roles), exploitation, abandonment or neglect, mentor incompetence (technically or relationally), boundary violations, problematic attraction, and unresolved disputes.

Although all mentors and mentorships are imperfect, competent mentors accept the reality of their own imperfection and diligently work to detect and address early on any indicators of distress and dissatisfaction they sense in their relationships with protégés. In this section, we discuss several key elements for handling mentorship difficulties. Our focus is on restoration and mentors should take the lead in restoring relationships. However, when a mentorship cannot be restored or when the continuing relationship is not in the protégé's best interest, mentors must take the lead in responsibly ending the relationship.

48
Above All, Do No Harm

Although the mentorship between Glen, a senior editor at a New York publisher, and Rick, a junior editorial assistant at the firm, began normally and was initially quite helpful to Rick and enjoyable to Glen, things took a turn for the worse when personality differences began to surface. Aggressive and ambitious by nature, Glen was a certified "workaholic." He frequently worked 70-hour weeks, was highly attuned to the power dynamics in the firm, and worked hard to compete against other editors for resources and prestigious projects. Although Glen expected the same of his protégés, he soon realized that Rick lacked aggressiveness and favored more moderate work hours. Rick was competent and appeared to enjoy his work, but obviously he was disinterested in "beating out" his peers for promotions. An experienced mentor, Glen noticed himself becoming increasingly short-tempered and even disgusted with Rick's low-key and noncompetitive style. After some self-reflection, Glen realized he was most helpful to protégés who, like him, were driven, ambitious, and willing to "fight" their way to the top. Aware that these personality differences and his own low frustration tolerance were beginning to interfere with the mentorship and place Rick at risk for

receiving unhelpful criticism and disdain from his mentor, Glen openly discussed
the problem of match with Rick and worked to find a better-suited editor with
whom Rick could begin working. To his credit, Glen was careful to protect Rick
from negative career outcomes and from mentor abandonment.

Mentors may not be able to *fix* every problem in their mentorships. Some problems are just too big, deep, or serious to handle. As much as possible, though, they can minimize the damage. The medical profession understands the importance of damage control. Physicians the world over swear by the Hippocratic Oath, which begins with the sage warning: "First, do no harm."

Avoiding harm is called *nonmaleficence*. It is the most fundamental ethical obligation mentors have to their protégés. Nonmaleficence also may be the most difficult ethical obligation to uphold. A souring mentorship can get extremely complicated, befuddling even the most astute mentor. There are numerous ways to harm a protégé. Certainly, a protégé can be harmed emotionally or physically. An angry tirade, bitter criticism, or chronic disparagement laced with profanity will take a toll on even the most resilient protégé. More often, however, harm accrues insidiously, at times without conscious awareness. When a protégé is neglected and ignored, tasked with challenges for which he or she is ill-prepared, sacrificed on the altar of organizational politics, or forced to relinquish creativity and individuality to appease the mentor, a protégé is harmed.

How do mentors avoid harm? Here are four guidelines. First, as the primary power-holder in the mentorship, mentors own the responsibility for ensuring that the mentorship benefits (versus harms) the protégé. They do not turn that responsibility over to the protégé. Second, mentors must set as priority the professional and developmental needs of the protégé. Certainly, mentors do not deny their own needs. They simply do not allow mentoring to become "win-lose"—the mentor winning and the protégé losing. Third, mentors continue to treat protégés with dignity, respect, and compassion even when protégés disappoint them. Particularly when a mentor feels wronged or disappointed, it may be easy to unwittingly step out of the professional role and cause harm to the protégé through an angry outburst or sudden abandonment. If a mentor becomes personally impacted or outraged such that respect gives way to disrespect, the mentor more than likely should stop mentoring. Finally, mentors stay committed to the protégé but accountable to the organization. They serve the protégé's best interests and they remain loyal and truthful to them. At the same time, they uphold obligations imposed by the sponsoring organization or profession. For example, a manager in an assigned mentorship would work to provide objective evaluations of a protégé and perhaps arrange for a smooth transfer when it becomes clear that the relationship is either unhelpful or destructive.

Key Components

- *Avoid harming your protégé either overtly or subtly.*
- *Take responsibility for ensuring that the mentorship benefits the protégé.*
- *Place your protégé's developmental needs before your own.*
- *Treat protégés with dignity, respect, and compassion—even when they are disappointing.*
- *Protect your protégé while honoring obligations to the organization and profession.*

49
Slow Down the Process

When June began working for a large commercial real-estate firm, she was impressed by Kathy, an experienced agent and manager. During June's first year in the firm, she looked for opportunities to work closely with Kathy and was delighted when Kathy began offering her career advice and involving June as an assistant in various managerial tasks. Things went smoothly until Kathy discovered that June had been gossiping about her to others in the firm—suggesting that Kathy was a "dinosaur" and that Kathy's business techniques were archaic and unnecessarily costly. Enraged, Kathy regretted the time she had invested in June and she had an impulse to both confront June angrily and sabotage her career. Instead, she took several days to "cool off," collect first-hand accounts from other managers, and carefully prepare for a discussion with June. Through this decelerated process, Kathy discovered that the reports of June's behavior were exaggerated. She was able to calmly and clearly express disappointment to June and request that any further concerns be addressed to her directly. Although this event marked a muting in the mentorship's intensity, Kathy's ability to control her impulse prevented a permanent fracture in the relationship.

When things go wrong, the events that take place can feel like they are on *fast forward.* Dominos of emotion and reaction cascade right in front of you. Before you realize what is really taking place, problems in the mentorship escalate, unanticipated and deep emotions surface, and both parties begin to question how they ever got into the situation in the first place. In this atmosphere of turbulence, mentors cannot afford to have knee-jerk reactions or brush the problems aside. Neither is acceptable. Before they do anything, mentors should deliberately engage in thoughtful reflection, analysis, and consultation.

When mentors have quick and thoughtless responses to conflict or dysfunctional protégé behavior, the reactions may worsen the already tenuous situation. When mentors avoid addressing difficulties with protégés, these reactions may also exacerbate conflict and ultimately ensure the demise of the mentorship. Common forms of dysfunctional mentor behavior include both self-defeating *provocation* and self-defeating *passivity.* The provocative mentor swiftly vents anger and frustration in a highly emotional and accusing manner—typically ensuring that the protégé responds in kind or emotionally withdraws from the mentorship. Furthermore, some mentors become active saboteurs; they betray the protégé or seek to harm them professionally as a means of exacting revenge.

The passively self-defeating mentor may engage in one of three unhelpful responses in the face of negative emotion or conflict. These include *paralysis* (the mentor freezes and fails to respond at all), *distancing* (the mentor intentionally disengages from the relationship and avoids the protégé altogether), and *appeasement* (the mentor passively capitulates, giving the protégé whatever he or she demands in hopes of diffusing conflict and restoring equilibrium). Each of these provocative and passive reactions is ultimately destined to worsen mentorship dysfunction and none offer the protégé an adaptive example of professional conflict management.

Instead of responding impulsively or avoiding problems altogether, effective mentors engage in a deliberate process of analysis, reflection, and when needed, consultation. They begin by listening carefully to the protégé's concerns or exploring the source of their own dissatisfaction or anger. They then consider their obligations to the protégé (e.g., do no harm, serve the protégé's best interests) and whether any ethical or professional standards have a bearing on the situation. Most importantly, the wise mentor uses this self-reflective time to honestly evaluate his or her own contribution to the current dysfunction; how has the mentor's behavior shaped the current state of affairs? When the causes of mentorship disturbance are clarified and the best interests of the protégé considered, the mentor explores possible solutions and the potential consequences of each. Ultimately, the mentor decides on a course of action he or she deems most likely to further the growth and development of the protégé while simultaneously resolving or reducing the current relationship disturbance.

Key Components

- *Take time to cool off and reflect before responding to problems or conflict with a protégé.*
- *Avoid provoking your protégé through angry outbursts or acts of revenge.*
- *Refuse to use passive strategies (paralysis, distancing) in the face of conflict.*
- *Examine the sources of dysfunction including your contribution(s).*
- *Seek solutions that serve your protégé's best interests.*

50
Tell the Truth

When Kathleen, a professor of psychology, admitted Chris to a very competitive research-oriented doctoral program, she had high hopes that Chris would excel in his studies and go on to become a faculty member at a prestigious university. Over time, however, Kathleen found Chris to be only moderately motivated and prone to mediocre work. As Chris's mentor, other faculty approached Kathleen about Chris's substandard performance in their courses. Further, Chris was frequently late with assignments and neglected important research tasks in Kathleen's lab. Although Kathleen mentioned these concerns to Chris and attempted to help him develop very specific short-term goals and study habits, he continued to perform poorly. At the end of Chris's second year of study, Kathleen arranged a formal meeting and discussed Chris's well-documented shortcomings as a student. She was careful to emphasize her positive regard for Chris and to highlight his relative strengths. Nonetheless, Kathleen informed Chris that she could not continue to support him. Initially shocked, Chris admitted his ambivalence about graduate school and expressed appreciation for Kathleen's support and honesty.

When things go wrong with a protégé, a mentor can always make things worse. The mentor could decide to not discuss the problem, address it superficially, or be untruthful. All of these tactics are really forms of avoidance. But a mentor should always try to make things better.

Just as mentors must take the lead in clarifying expectations with the protégé early in the relationship, they must take responsibility for alerting the protégé to early signs of relationship and performance problems. The alert should be direct and constructive. When a mentor avoids communicating complaints to the protégé he or she harbors a hidden agenda—one that is likely to re-emerge in the form of neglect or hostility. When a mentor attempts to communicate concerns about the protégé through subtle innuendo or nonverbal cues, he or she is actually acting as an enabler of a dysfunctional and stagnant mentorship. Obviously, a mentor should model an appropriate strategy by being an agent of positive change and health.

Some mentors find honesty difficult, especially when it requires delivery of unfavorable feedback. In fact, some deeply caring and technically competent mentors are chronically dishonest in this regard. They withhold critical feedback—information that is often essential for growth, change, and long-term success. Whether phobic about confrontation, fearful of hurting feelings, or anxious about rejection, these mentors fail at truth-telling and do a profound disservice to those they mentor. Inadvertently, they allow self-defeating protégé behavior to continue and they worsen existing mentorship problems.

Experience suggests and research confirms that when a mentor–protégé pair experience conflict, resentment, or dissatisfaction, the relationship is most likely to be restored and strengthened when the mentor expresses concerns about the problem. For such overt and clear communication to be successful, the mentor must typically plan the meeting or discussion with the protégé. When confrontation is required, it behooves the mentor to remain both kind and concrete. This should hold true even when confronting a protégé for significant errors, performance difficulties, or disloyal behavior. The wise mentor balances confrontation with compassion. Before launching into the protégé's problem areas, mentors typically begin a confrontational meeting with some reflection on the protégé's strengths and assets. This approach helps mentors convey a balanced picture of the protégé.

Key Components

- *Do not withhold honest and constructive feedback.*
- *Raise relationship or performance concerns immediately so they can be contained and addressed.*
- *Be direct and forthright when confronting problems, recognizing that passivity and innuendo are destructive.*
- *Plan feedback sessions carefully and always begin with the positive aspects of the protégé's personhood and performance.*

51
Seek Consultation

A full professor and seasoned medical school faculty member, Larry enjoyed career success, prestige, and considerable admiration from a generation of medical school students and junior faculty. A gifted mentor, Larry derived considerable pleasure from guiding and supporting new medical school professors who were under his supervision. On occasion, Larry developed particularly bonded relationships with assistant professors who showed exceptional promise and strong interest in being mentored. Audrey was this kind of protégé. During Audrey's first two years on faculty, the two developed a very close and productive mentoring connection. Gradually, however, Larry noticed steadily accelerating feelings of emotional and romantic attraction to Audrey. He also noticed that Audrey appeared less comfortable around him at times and that he had been attempting to schedule "lunch meetings" with greater frequency. Troubled by this awareness, Larry con-

tacted a good colleague at another medical school, sharing information about the mentorship scenario and his own feelings while protecting Audrey's identity. Larry was both comforted by his friend's support and reinforced in his resolve to protect the professional nature of the relationship. Although the two agreed that it was unwise and unnecessary to discuss his feelings with Audrey, it was important for Larry to remain self-aware, decrease the frequency of his meetings with Audrey, and to keep their conversations focused on career-helping. Larry also agreed to "check-in" with his colleague for consultation every couple of months. These boundary-maintenance strategies helped Larry to refocus. Audrey appeared to respond positively to the changes.

No one can be expected to have the solutions to every problem. Sometimes mentors themselves need help, especially when they are dealing with complex ethical issues or vexing personal reactions. Under normal circumstances, ethical decision-making can be complicated. It can feel overwhelming when influenced by biased perceptions, strong emotions, or confusion regarding the best interests of the protégé. For example, when a mentor has been consistently disappointed by a protégé and wonders about a protégé's ability to succeed in the profession, when a protégé appears to harbor antisocial or unethical attitudes and behaviors, or when a mentor feels strongly attracted to a protégé and is close to romanticizing or sexualizing a mentorship, it is often difficult to sort out an appropriate and ethical response.

Mentors who seek consultation from trusted colleagues are consistently likely to make better decisions than those who do not. They are more inclined to proceed ethically and professionally in a troubling or challenging mentorship. When choosing a consultant, look for a seasoned colleague known for a strong commitment to the profession, sensitivity to ethical matters, and a reputation for being both forthright and discrete. The last quality is important in safeguarding confidentiality in mentorships. Your success as a mentor will hinge on your reputation for protecting the privacy and confidence of your protégés. Therefore, exercise discretion regarding with whom you consult. Also, protect the anonymity of the protégé when this is warranted. One safeguard is to select a consultant in a different organization or distant geographic location. In smaller organizations, this may be the only way to really protect protégé confidence.

Also, your own mentor may be the perfect confidant. Do not rule out your mentor even though the two of you are in the same organization. A trusted mentor may be ideally suited to understanding mentorship dynamics and care for you in the process of advice giving. In this way a mentor's legacy may be extended to more distant generations of protégés.

Excellent mentors use occasional consultation to develop a balanced and reasonable strategy for confronting protégés, handling ethical or legal issues, or developing clearer insight about a confusing relational dynamic. Consultation is particularly important if a mentor feels threatened or over-whelmed at the prospect of confronting a protégé or if the mentor has acted inappropriately and requires assistance in formulating a professional approach to restore the relationship. Finally, we cannot overemphasize the importance of using good peer consultation to explore one's own contri-butions to difficulties with protégés. Emotional problems (e.g., impulsive anger, neediness), personality traits (e.g., rigidity, narcissism), or manage-ment difficulties (e.g., becoming over-extended and unable to attend to protégés) all contribute to mentorship problems. Good mentors use self-reflection and consultation to understand and modify these characteristics.

Key Components

- *Seek consultation from a trusted colleague when a mentorship has be-come complicated, concerning, or conflicted.*
- *Select a seasoned colleague with good judgment, ethical commitment, and track record of discretion.*
- *Protect your protégé's privacy and identity by masking identifying in-formation.*
- *Use consultation to formulate a protégé–oriented response.*
- *Explore your own contributions to difficulties with protégés.*

52
Document Carefully

As vice president for operations at a large manufacturing company, Clark was an effective mentor to several junior managers. As a new mid-level manager in the company, Tom came to Clark's attention. He was ambitious, hard-charging, and eager to respond to Clark's advice and attention. As a mentorship developed, Clark began a small file containing notes on Tom's achievements and projects. He also noted important exchanges between the two of them and recommendations he had offered. Maintaining a file was standard practice for Clark who found these records very useful when writing future letters of recommendation for his protégés. During Tom's third month on the job, several red flags began to appear. First, several supervising managers noted that Tom had a tendency to be abrasive, arrogant, and too demanding—certainly not the type of behavior you expect of a junior manager, especially someone who is unproven. He became enraged when anyone questioned his decisions and sullen if another manager was singled out for praise. When Clark brought these concerns to his protégé's attention, he was met with angry accusations that he was "just like the others." Clark carefully documented these exchanges as well as comments and complaints from other managers. Two months later Tom was passed over for a promotion, reacting in his customary rage, accusing Clark of "sabotage," and deciding to file a suit against the company. Although he was shaken by this drama, Clark's detailed documentation of his attempts to mentor Tom proved essential in successfully defending the company.

You never know when documentation will come in handy. It might even save a lot of grief and misunderstanding. Clear documentation of one's rationale and approach to responding to mentorship dysfunction—particularly when the relationship has thoroughly unraveled—is often the best defense against vindictive protégé behavior or inaccurate accusations.

In very rare circumstances, a mentorship may fall apart. Although there are many potential sources of mentorship conflict, the most common—discussed at the start of this section—include faulty communication, neglect of a protégé, unresolved disagreements, perceived disloyalty, violations of professional boundaries, and some measure of pathology or character disturbance on the part of either the mentor or protégé. Whatever the cause, excellent mentors work to diffuse hostility, correct misunderstandings, and reconcile differences in mentor relationships.

When it becomes apparent that a mentorship cannot be salvaged and that continuation is either impossible or likely to result in additional negative outcomes, either party may terminate the relationship (this sometimes occurs indirectly if a protégé simply refuses further contact with a mentor). On rare occasions, a protégé may gossip about a former mentor or even file a formal complaint in an effort to exact emotional retribution or sabotage a mentor's career. In these cases, a mentor will be well served if he or she has carefully documented the development of the conflict. In addition to the mentor's own narrative, excellent documentation will include evidence of reflection about the problem, efforts to address the conflict and restore the relationship, any collegial consultation, thoughts about ethical duties and professional requirements, and overarching evidence of concern for the protégé's best interests.

Finally, it is important to note that documentation should not only be seen as an emergency tool for responding defensively to protégé complaints. Routine documentation of ongoing mentorships is also encouraged as an indicator of intentional and deliberate mentoring excellence. Brief but clear documentation of mentorship formation, early discussions of relationship expectations, and periodic assessments of the mentorship's benefits and outcomes signal to both the protégé and external observers that the mentor is thoughtful and intentional about the mentoring enterprise. Conflict aside, a well-documented mentorship also makes positive mentoring tasks more effective and efficient. For example, when asked to write letters of recommendation for a previous protégé, a small folder of documentation will prove invaluable and will allow you to construct a thorough and accurate picture of your protégé.

Key Components

- *Document your mentorships carefully as a way of ensuring good practice and protecting yourself and your protégés from subsequent misrepresentation of the relationship.*
- *Practice terse record-keeping of protégé goals, expectations, achievements, and concerns.*
- *Record instances of conflict or negative interactions as well as clear rationale and description of your response.*
- *Document consultation and efforts to provide corrective feedback and restore the relationship.*

53
Dispute Your Irrational Thinking

As head of a large federal agency, Sandy was a case-study in professional and managerial success. In Kathryn, a new managerial trainee and a fresh college graduate, Sandy saw a mirror image of herself three decades earlier. Kathryn was smart, interpersonally savvy, and quite ambitious. These qualities prompted Sandy to take Kathryn under her wing, beginning what would become a very meaningful mentoring relationship. Things began to change during Kathryn's third year with the agency. Recently married, she began dropping hints about taking time off to have a family or perhaps even changing careers to something less demanding. Although she was happy for Kathryn on one level, Sandy found herself reacting to Kathryn with anger, annoyance, and stern warnings about "throwing away a promising career to change diapers." After one particularly terse conversation, Sandy was startled by the vehemence of her own comments and the intensity of her powerful feelings of disappointment and betrayal. Upon some difficult reflection, Sandy realized she was making several rather extreme evaluations of Kathryn and Kathryn's choices. Some of Sandy's irrational thoughts and demands were: "She should follow my career path and model my example precisely," "she must see that I know best and take my advice," "it is awful and catastrophic that this bright young woman might squander a fine career opportunity!" Not only did Sandy recognize these thoughts and evaluations as extreme, she shared her insights with Kathryn and was able to both laugh at herself and give Kathryn permission to make her own decisions with Sandy's blessing. Ultimately, Kathryn stayed with the agency, worked half-time for several years, and enjoyed a successful managerial career. The mentorship was bolstered by Sandy's insight and willingness to change her "crazy thinking."

When things go wrong in a mentorship, mentors need to know what part they play in the disturbance. They need to ask themselves these questions. "How am I making myself disturbed?" "How is my disturbance interfering with the relationship?" "How can I get beyond the disturbance?"

At times, even the most mature, rational, and seasoned mentor falls prey to pernicious and destructive irrational beliefs. Irrational beliefs are rigid—though often unconscious—demands about self, the protégé, or the relationship. Irrational demands almost always lead to additional irrational thinking such as harsh evaluations (e.g., "My protégé is absolutely worthless and should suffer for causing me so much extra work!"), catastrophic thinking (e.g., "This is absolutely awful!"), and poor frustration tolerance (e.g., "I can't stand this!"). Strong irrational beliefs nearly always lead to emotional upset (e.g., anger, anxiety, depression) and usually make matters with protégés much worse. It may not be surprising that the type of person most likely to become an excellent mentor (e.g., successful, achievement-focused, driven to help others) may be more prone to adopt certain self-defeating irrational tendencies. This type of driven individual sometimes pushes the envelope in his or her thinking patterns.

Examples of irrational beliefs most likely to plague otherwise fine mentors are: (a) I *must* be successful with all of my protégés all of the time; (b) I *have* to be greatly respected and loved by all of my protégés; (c) Because I have invested so much as a mentor, my protégés *should* be equally ambitious and always eager to do exactly what I recommend; (d) I *must* reap tremendous benefit from mentoring and should enjoy mentoring all the time; and (e) My protégés *must* never leave or disappoint me. Quite often, when mentors are upset and disturbed with either a protégé or with themselves as a mentor, one of these irrational demands bubbles to the top and interferes with resolution and restoration.

In spite of the human proclivity for irrational self-disturbance, excellent mentors adopt several strategies for minimizing the negative impact of irrational thinking. Mentor coping strategies include: (a) acknowledging disturbance and upset while searching for one's contributing irrational demands and evaluations; (b) actively disputing or challenging mentor-related irrational beliefs in front of one's protégés (e.g., "You know, when you neglected to turn in that report as promised, I really got myself enraged at first. Then I realized I was crazily demanding that you be perfect. Now I'm just a bit annoyed and wondering how I can help you get that report wrapped up"); (c) refuse to tell yourself that anything a protégé does (or fails to do) is awful; (d) carefully separate human worth (your own and the protégé's) from performance; and (e) frequently and humorously find opportunities to display your own fallibility (thus providing a good model of human imperfection for the protégé).

Key Components

- *Recognize your irrational demands of protégés and evaluations of events.*

- *Be alert to signs that you are harshly evaluating, exaggerating, or failing to tolerate frustration.*

- *Actively dispute dysfunctional beliefs about protégés, yourself as mentor, and the ideal mentorship.*

- *Disclose irrational thinking to protégés, laugh at yourself, and show protégés how you correct your own self-defeating thinking.*

Welcoming Change
and Saying Goodbye

Matters of Closure

Many mentorships end with unfinished business. Healthy closure of a mentorship is rare. Mentors either fail to understand the necessity of planning to end the mentorship on a positive note or actively avoid the pain and sadness that sometimes accompany saying goodbye.

Ours is a culture of pain avoidance. Because relationship endings can be painful—particularly when a mentor and protégé have become closely bonded and the relationship is especially meaningful—the intuitive human response is to avoid the discomfort of loss. In his Pulitzer Prize winning book, *The Denial of Death*, Ernest Becker makes the case that human beings phobically and unconsciously avoid basic awareness, let alone active consideration, of the reality of the end of life. Along similar lines, human beings—including seasoned and intelligent professionals who mentor—often avoid the reality of the death of a relationship. In our experience, too many mentors are poor at managing the final phase of mentoring. There are three primary reasons why mentors fail at this task. First, many people never had graceful endings modeled in their own relationships with mentors. As a result, they do not have a picture of how a healthy ending looks. Second, many people come from family and cultural backgrounds where denial of endings is the norm. When a close friend moves away, people are comfortable saying "see you around" and then they get back to work. Finally, some mentors simply find it threatening when a protégé leaves. As the protégé pulls away and disengages, mentors may have a host of reactions, including self-protective anger or reactive disengagement. This may bring otherwise good mentorships to pathetic termination.

Mindful mentors understand the importance of preparing for meaningful closure of the mentorship. They come to celebrate protégé transitions and leave-taking. Rather than allowing a long-term mentor relationship to end suddenly or fade away unacknowledged, they make the interior world of thought and emotion explicit in a way that brings meaningful closure for both parties. Because of their appreciation of the *redefinition* phase, they actively arrange opportunities and venues for open discussion of the experience of ending. Great mentors find ways to honor and mark the protégé's increasing autonomy, the decreasing intensity of the mentorship, and the pending end of the mentorship's active phase. A self-aware mentor might express gratitude for the privilege of knowing the protégé, sadness at seeing the protégé move on, and deep satisfaction at the protégé's competence and confidence. When a mentor models open acknowledgment of relational transitions and endings, protégés are blessed. Permission is granted for the protégé to move on. Such experiences are deeply meaningful to protégés and reaffirm the value of the mentorship for the long term.

In this section we highlight the importance of welcoming protégé development, accepting and embracing the end of relationships, discovering helpful ways to say goodbye, and becoming a mentor as a way of life.

54
Welcome Change and Growth

When Bob transferred to the company's marketing division, Gale liked him immediately. A senior marketing team manager, Gale was delighted to have a bright and energetic trainee with whom to share his experience and marketing savvy. Inquisitive by nature and eager to watch Gale at work, Bob proved to be a quick study and he soon was making valuable contributions to the creative team's brainstorming sessions and marketing research. Within the year, Gale was including Bob in all of the company's marketing projects and their relationship flourished. During Bob's third year with the team, Gale realized that Bob needed less career advice and very little direct supervision. Bob actually began to outpace Gale. He became more productive and creative. Initially, Gale was threatened and disheartened. In Gale's mind, mentors are supposed to outpace protégés. Eventually, Gale realized Bob's success was at least partially related to their good mentorship. With this realization, Gale began commenting on Bob's professional growth, and the changing nature of their connection—from mentorship to collegial friendship. These efforts heightened Bob's confidence as well as his appreciation for Gale's support.

All relationships evolve and change. If the changes are not fruitful, stagnation or deterioration set in, signaling something is drastically wrong in the mentorship. By their nature, mentorships are developmental relationships, focused on the transition of the protégé from neophyte to full member of a profession. Mentors should remember, though, that mentorships grow at different rates—each according to a number of factors. Expectations vary. Although change is a requisite of healthy mentoring, there is tremendous variation in the rate or trajectory of change. Some protégés race to test their skills as independent professionals, while others are timid and reluctant. Some mentors are better facilitators of change than others. Although growth and change are the very essence of mentoring, some pain and adjustment inevitably accompany mentorship transitions. One time when pain is particularly noticeable is when the protégé begins the process of separating from the mentor. Both parties may experience turmoil, anxiety, loss, and general disruption. Either party may consciously or unconsciously resist the change—clinging to the way things used to be. For example, in an effort to preserve a valued relationship, a mentor may ignore the fundamental ethical requirement to promote protégé autonomy and independence, opting instead to foster dependency and withhold endorsement of the protégé's competence.

Management professor Kathy Kram identified four common phases of mentorship development. Excellent mentors should become familiar with these phases, understand the unique needs of protégés in each phase, and acknowledge and welcome transition to a new phase. The first phase of mentorship development, *initiation,* is marked by excitement, possibility, and beginning. The protégé often feels anxious, overwhelmed and quite dependent on the mentor. New protégés may feel unqualified and inadequate professionally—an imposter waiting to be revealed. Although protégés usually are open to feedback, are coachable and enjoyable to work with during this phase, mentors must be cautious not to encourage protégés to clone themselves in the image of the mentor.

Phase two, *cultivation,* typically begins after several months and is often the most productive phase of the mentorship. During this period, which often lasts at least a year or two, protégés demonstrate increasing competence and confidence. They begin to establish a personal professional identity—often assimilating their mentor's example into their own personal style. During this phase, it is essential for the mentor to entrust the protégé with increasing responsibility and autonomy. Mentors must also allow the relationship to become increasingly reciprocal and collegial.

In the third phase, *separation,* the mentorship is characterized by leave-taking and distancing. This may be a difficult time emotionally as both parties must accept some loss and arrange to say goodbye to the intensive phase of the relationship. As the mentorship becomes (appropriately) less central in the life of the protégé, a mentor may experience loss, anger, or even insecurity at the protégé's new competence. Excellent mentors work through these feelings, intentionally endorse the protégé's status as colleague, and reinforce the protégé's sense of autonomy.

Whatever the phase of mentorship development or the rate of protégé growth, the important thing is for the mentor to welcome change. It is helpful for the mentor to take the lead in occasionally discussing the status of the mentorship. Important questions to ask are as follows: How far has the protégé come and where is he or she going? Are there noticeable changes in the nature of the relationship, the protégé's competence, and the mentor's view of the protégé as professional? Good mentors celebrate growth and change with their protégés even when change brings about loss. They understand that celebration is a memorable marker of transition.

Key Components

- *Accept the fact that good mentoring will ensure growth in your protégé and change in your relationship.*

- *Recognize that development and independence in protégés requires you to tolerate some sadness and make adjustments.*
- *Understand the common phases of mentorship development and how your protégé might need different things from you at each phase.*
- *Narrate, welcome, and even highlight evidence of protégé independence.*

55
Accept Endings

Myrna was sometimes humorously referred to as the "Czar" of the university's chemistry department. As the department chair and faculty leader for nearly two decades, Myrna was a trove of wisdom and a force to be reckoned with when it came to policy and decision making. Myrna was particularly fond of mentoring some of her most promising young faculty. Over the years, she had become acquainted with the common seasons of mentorships and had learned, sometimes painfully, to anticipate and even welcome significant changes and transitions in the lives of these treasured relationships. Although Myrna had been most troubled by the separation phase of mentorships with students and faculty early in her career, she had learned—the hard way in some instances—that reluctance to let a protégé mature and become independent was a sure fire way to stifle growth or place protégés in a painful double-bind (either remain dependent and highly connected or break away from the mentor entirely). As a result, Myrna had become proactive in anticipating and openly acknowledging the separation and redefinition seasons of mentorships. She acknowledged the mixed experience of sadness and satisfaction at seeing skilled faculty move on in their careers and she found creative and meaningful rituals for marking these transitions.

The final phase of mentorship development is called the *redefinition* phase. After the more difficult separation phase, mentor and protégé may continue a collegial friendship characterized by less frequent and informal contact. As the protégé achieves peer status with the mentor, he or she often feels gratitude and appreciation for the mentor's guidance, while the mentor continues to support the protégé's career and take pride in the protégé's accomplishments.

This ideal outcome requires both mentor and protégé to work through any strong feeling associated with ending the working phase of the mentorship. Outstanding mentors help protégés articulate and work through feelings of sadness or anxiety associated with letting go. Simultaneously, they acknowledge and manage their own sadness, anger, or anxiety at the prospect of losing such an important and close professional connection. In the worst cases, both mentor and protégé may collude to avoid the subject of termination altogether, attempting to go on as if no change has occurred and as if the protégé will require the mentor's intense intervention forever. Such collusion, of course, serves to stunt the protégé's growth and ultimately reduce the value of the mentorship.

Healthy mentors appreciate the seasons of a mentoring relationship. They anticipate and gracefully tolerate relationship transitions and take the lead in discussing these with their protégés. Healthy mentors accept endings when mentorships have run their course and facilitate closure when it is time for a protégé to move on and function independently. Excellent mentors help their protégés to appreciate the past but also welcome the future. They help protégés see that the end of the active phase of a mentorship signals success and that any other outcome would be cause for concern.

Key Components

- *Work hard at recognizing and accepting mentorship transitions and endings.*
- *Allow yourself to accept and experience sadness and loss when a particularly close mentorship becomes less active and requires redefinition.*
- *Model acceptance of ending for protégés and initiate explicit discussions about how each party experiences relationship changes.*
- *Reframe endings as inevitable and indicative of mentorship success.*

56
Find Helpful Ways to Say Goodbye

After five years of mentoring Adrian, Sam had come to see her as part managerial superstar in the making, part creative colleague, and part beloved "daughter." Sam had recognized Adrian's unusual leadership talent during her first year with the company and had chosen her from a vast pool of junior managers to become the assistant vice president of human relations. In this role, Adrian had flourished—at least partly as a result of Sam's strong advocacy, coaching, and protection. Adrian's work had begun to attract the attention of other vice presidents and the board of directors. She was soon offered a major promotion and a vice presidency of a division. Though surprised by his own ambivalence at her success (delighted for her success yet deeply saddened by her departure), Sam recognized both the importance of this promotion for Adrian's career and the difficulty she was having sharing her decision to move on with him. To give her permission to move on, and simultaneously, to recognize an important transition in the mentorship, Sam scheduled a lunch meeting with Adrian. During the meeting, he offered a retrospective of their mentorship, starting with his early perceptions of her unique talents, his delight in their synergistic and creative working relationship, and his pleasure and pride in her remarkable accomplishments. He emphasized the ways in which the mentorship had been helpful professionally and meaningful personally. Sam also acknowledged the ending of the active phase of their mentorship and described his mixture of sadness and gratitude at coming to this transition. This parting ritual proved profoundly meaningful to Adrian who was freed to express her own ambivalence about leaving and her deep appreciation for Sam's graceful support. Their contact grew less frequent, but they continued to support each other for years.

Preparing to say goodbye to a protégé is among the most often overlooked yet richly satisfying elements of successful mentoring. Quite often, only the most seasoned mentors carefully honor endings. Excellent mentors find creative methods for recognizing and honoring good collaboration, strong friendship, and important professional growth in a protégé. Such recognition is particularly important at salient transitions points between phases in a mentorship or when a mentorship has run its course and is moving toward long-term ending or redefinition. Saying goodbye requires self-awareness and the ability to both experience and articulate feelings about the protégé and about allowing the protégé to move on.

One of the most effective methods of bringing closure to a mentorship is to schedule a formal time to process and celebrate the protégé's moving on. This may take the form of a lunch or dinner meeting or just a conversation over a cup of coffee. A formal meeting offers the mentor an opportunity to say goodbye to the protégé through the medium of story-telling; the mentor offers a narrative of the mentorship including salient highlights of the protégé's developmental milestones and things about the protégé that have most impressed the mentor. By weaving the history of the mentorship into a coherent narrative, the mentor allows the protégé to clearly reflect on his or her growth and accomplishments through the lens of the mentor.

The mentor may also helpfully disclose his or her own feelings about the mentorship, the protégé, and about the pending transition or ending. By giving voice to important emotions and experiences, the mentor frees the protégé to do the same. In many cases, a protégé will avoid formally saying goodbye to a mentor unless the mentor takes the lead—offering a model of how to do this well. As mentor and protégé share reflections and express gratitude for one another, relationship closure occurs. Both parties are free to take leave, redefine the relationship, and move forward with new endeavors and perhaps different mentorships.

Key Components

- *Say goodbye to your protégé and explicitly acknowledge the end of a mentorship.*
- *Arrange a specific meeting or interaction for the purpose of saying goodbye and formally recognizing change in the relationship.*
- *Provide your protégé with a personal narrative of the mentorship, including your feelings and thoughts about the protégé.*
- *Be sure to acknowledge intangible gifts received and lessons learned from the protégé.*

57
Mentor as a Way of Life

Although he had been retired from the school district for nearly ten years, Henry continued to serve as coach, confidant, encourager, and sponsor to several gener-

ations of high school students, teachers, and administrators. During a 40-year career in education, Henry had gone from first-year science teacher to becoming the first African American principal of the largest high school in the state. Naturally inclined to helping juniors, Henry was beloved by several generations of African American men and women whom he mentored in the teaching profession. Many had become successful administrators, emulating their mentor. Known for his open-door policy, keen interpersonal skills, and genuine interest in the lives of his students and teachers, Henry had profoundly touched the lives of hundreds of protégés. Although happy to give up his administrative duties at retirement, Henry continued to savor relationships with younger teachers and the opportunity to share his wisdom and propel their careers through letters of recommendation, sponsorship, and support. Although Henry's wife was sometimes frustrated at his continued involvement in the lives of his many protégés, he derived great satisfaction from developing talent in others. Henry remained a powerful and influential mentor to young educators until his death.

Authentic mentors never stop mentoring. Over the years, mentoring becomes a deeply engrained and consistently expressed facet of the mentor's personality. Seldom will the master mentor's inclinations toward helping lie dormant or untapped.

Research indicates that excellent mentors manifest a general personality tendency or interest in caring for younger and less experienced individuals. This is often referred to as *generative concern*. Generative concern cannot be taught or trained. It either exists in the fundamental core of the mentor's personality or it does not. Mentors who are generative and caring by nature are those who endure in the mentor role. Not surprisingly, generativity is strongly related to openness, emotional stability, and agreeableness. These mentors often help scores of protégés during their lifetime and many of their mentorships continue as strong collegial friendships for years.

Mentoring becomes a way of life for outstanding mentors—both because they delight in seeing protégés succeed and because they reap rich internal rewards. Research on generative men and women show that they report greater levels of happiness and general life satisfaction. So automatic is the tendency to mentor in these generative souls that not mentoring is never a viable consideration. Although mentors choose protégés selectively and safeguard their own time and resources for protégés, it is difficult for the generative mentor not to mentor. Remember, however, that you can't mentor everyone. To successfully mentor across an entire career, return to our very first element: set limits and be selective.

Key Components

- *Make mentoring a common component of your ongoing life and work.*
- *Remember that if you are drawn to mentoring, you probably have gifts in this area that will be best served by frequent use.*
- *Recognize the rich rewards associated with mentoring but take care to protect yourself from becoming overextended.*

References

Allen, T. D. (2003). Mentoring others: a dispositional and motivational approach. *Journal of Vocational Behavior* 62, 134–154.

Allen, T. D. & Poteet, M. L. (1999). Developing effective mentoring relationships: Strategies from the mentor's viewpoint. *The Career Development Quarterly* 48, 59–73.

Allen, T. D., Poteet, M. L., & Burroughs, S. M. (1997). The mentor's perspective: A qualitative inquiry and future research agenda. *Journal of Vocational Behavior* 51, 70–89.

Allen, T. D., Poteet, M. L., & Russell, J. E. A. (2000). Protégé selection by mentors: What makes the difference? *Journal of Organizational Behavior* 21, 271–282.

Ballantyne, R., Hansford, B., & Packer, J. (1995). Mentoring beginning teachers: A qualitative analysis of process and outcomes. *Educational Review* 47, 297–307.

Barnett, S. K. (1984). The mentor role: A task of generativity. *Journal of Human Behavior and Learning* 1, 15–18.

Bartell, P. A. & Rubin, L. J. (1990). Dangerous liaisons: Sexual intimacies in supervision. *Professional Psychology: Research and Practice* 21, 442–450.

Battle, A. & Wigfield, A. (2003). College women's value orientations toward family, career, and graduate school. *Journal of Vocational Behavior* 62, 56–75.

Becker, E. (1973). *The denial of death.* New York: The Free Press.

Bennett, R. & Knibbs, J. (1986). Researching for a higher degree: The role(s) of the supervisor. *Management Education and Development* 17, 137–145.

Blackburn, R. T., Chapman, D. W., & Cameron, S. M. (1981). "Cloning" in academia: Mentorship and academic careers. *Research in Higher Education* 15, 315–327.

Bolton, E. B. (1980). A conceptual analysis of the mentor relationship in the career development of women. *Adult Education* 30, 195–207.

Bowen, D. D. (1986). The role of identification in mentoring female protégés. *Groups & Organization Studies* 11, 61–74.

Bowlby, J. (1969). *Attachment and loss: Vol 1: Attachment.* New York: Basic Books.

Burke, R. J. (1984). Mentors in organizations. *Group and Organizational Studies* 9, 353–372.

Burke, R. J. & McKeen, C. A. (1997). Benefits of mentoring relationships among managerial and professional women: A cautionary tale. *Journal of Vocational Behavior* 51, 43–57.

Busch, J. W. (1985). Mentoring in graduate schools of education: Mentor's perceptions. *American Educational Research Journal* 22, 257–265.

Cameron, S. W. & Blackburn, R. T. (1981). Sponsorship and academic career success. *Journal of Higher Education* 52, 369–377.

Chao, G. T. (1997). Mentoring phases and outcomes. *Journal of Vocational Behavior* 51, 15–28.

Clawson, J. G. & Kram, K. E. (1984). Managing cross-gender mentoring. *Busniess Horizons* 27, 22–32.

Crosby, F. J. (1999). The developing literature on developmental relationships. In A. J. Murrell, F. J. Crosby, & R. J. Ely (eds.) *Mentoring dilemmas: Developmental relationships within multicultural organizations,* pp. 3–20. Mahwah, NJ: Lawrence Erlbaum.

Davis, J. & Rodela, E. S. (1992). Mentoring for the Hispanic: Mapping emotional support. In S. B. Knouse, P. Rosenfeld, & A. L. Culbertson (eds.), *Hispanics in the workplace,* pp. 151–169. Thousand Oaks, CA: Sage.

Davis, L. L., Litle, M. S., & Thornton, W. L. (1997). The art and angst of the mentoring relationship. *Academic Psychiatry* 21, 61–71.

Donaldson, S. I., Ensher, E. A., & Grant-Vallone, E. J. (2000). Longitudinal examination of mentoring relationships on organizational commitment and citizenship behavior. *Journal of Career Development* 26, 233–249.

Douglas, C. A. & McCauley, C. D. (1999). Formal developmental relationships: A survey of organizational practices. *Human Resource Development Quarterly* 10, 203–221.

Dreher, G. F. & Ash, R. A. (1990). A comparative study of mentoring among men and women in managerial, professional, and technical positions. *Journal of Applied Psychology* 75, 539–546.

Eby, L. T. & Allen, T. D. (2002). Further investigation of protégés' negative mentoring experiences: Patterns and outcomes. *Group and Organization Management* 27, 456–479.

Ellis, A. & Harper, R. A. (1975). *A new guide to rational living.* Hollywood, CA: Wilshire.

Ensher, E. A. & Murphy, S. E. (1997). Effects of race, gender, perceived similarity, and contact on mentor relationships. *Journal of Vocational Behavior* 50, 460–481.

Fagenson, E. A. (1989). The mentor advantage: Perceived career/job experiences of protégés versus non-protégés. *Journal of Organizational Behavior* 10, 309–320.

Fagenson, E. A. (1994). Perceptions of Protégés' vs Nonprotégés' relationships with their peers, superiors, and departments. *Journal of Vocational Behavior* 45, 55–78.

Fagenson-Eland, E. A., Marks, M. A., & Amendola, K. L. (1997). Perceptions of mentoring relationships, *Journal of Vocational Behavior* 51, 29–42.

Feldman, D. C. (1999). Toxic mentors or toxic protégés? A critical re-examination of dysfunctional mentoring. *Human Resources Management Review* 9, 247–278.

Flum, H. (2001). Relational dimensions in career development. *Journal of Vocational Behavior* 59, 1–16.

Gaskill, L. R. (1991). Same-sex and cross-sex mentoring of female protégés: A comparative analysis. *Career Development Quarterly* 40, 48–63.

Godschalk, V. M. & Sosik, J. J. (2000). Does mentor–protégé agreement on mentor leadership behavior influence the quality of a mentoring relationship? *Group and Organization Management* 25, 291–317.

Goleman, D. (1995). *Emotional intelligence.* New York: Bantam Books.

Green, S. G. & Bauer, T. N. (1995). Supervisory mentoring by advisers: Relationships with doctoral student potential, productivity, and commitment. *Personnel Psychology* 48, 537–561.

Hall, D. T. (1987). Careers and socialization. *Journal of Management* 13, 301–321.

Higgins, M. C. & Kram, K. E. (2001). Reconceptualizing mentoring at work: A developmental network perspective. *Academy of Management Review* 26, 264–288.

Higgins, M. C. & Thomas, D. A. (2001). Constellations and careers: Toward understanding the effects of multiple developmental relationships. *Journal of Organizational Behavior* 22, 223–247.

Hill, C. E. & O'Brien, K. M. (1999). *Helping skills: Facilitating exploration, insight, and action.* Washington, DC: American Psychological Association.

Hunt, D. M. & Michael, C. (1983). Mentorship: A career training and development tool. *Academy of Management Review* 8, 475–485.

Johnson, D. W. (1981). *Reaching out: Interpersonal effectiveness and self-actualization.* Englewood Cliffs, NJ: Prentice-Hall.

Johnson, W. B. (2002). The intentional mentor: Strategies and guidelines for the practice of mentoring. *Professional Psychology: Research and Practice* 33, 88–96.

Johnson, W. B. (2003). A framework for conceptualizing competence to mentor. *Ethics & Behavior* 13, 127–151.

Johnson, W. B. & Huwe, J. M. (2003) *Getting mentored in graduate school.* Washington, DC: American Psychological Association.

Johnson, W. B., Huwe, J. M., & Lucas, J. L. (2000). Rational mentoring. *Journal of Rational-Emotive and Cognitive-Behavior Therapy* 18, 39–54.

Johnson, W. B. & Nelson, N. (1999). Mentoring relationships in graduate training: Some ethical concerns. *Ethics and Behavior* 9, 189–210.

Kitchener, K. S. (1992). Psychologist as teacher and mentor: Affirming ethical values throughout the curriculum. *Professional Psychology: Research and Practice* 23, 190–195.

Kram, K. E. (1983). Phases of the mentor relationship. *Academy of Management Journal* 26 (4), 608–625.

Kram, K. E. (1985). *Mentoring at work: Developmental relationships in organizational life.* Glenview, ILL: Scott Foresman.

Kram, K. E. & Isabella, L. A. (1985). Mentoring alternatives: The role of peer relationships in career development. *Academy of Management Journal* 28, 110–132.

Levinson, D. J., Darrow, C. N., Klein, E. B., Levinson, M. H., & McKee, B. (1978). *The seasons of a man's life.* New York: Ballantine.

Nelson, M L. & Friedlander, M. L. (2001). A close look at conflictual supervisory relationships: The trainee's perspective. *Journal of Counseling Psychology* 48, 384–395.

Newby, T. J. & Heide, A. (1992). The value of mentoring. *Performance Improvement Quarterly* 5, 2–15.

Noe, R. A. (1988). Women and mentoring: A review and research agenda. *Academy of Management Review* 13, 65–78.

Noe, R. A., Greenberger, D. B., & Wang, S. (2003). Mentoring: What we know and where we might go. *Research in Personnel and Human Resources Management* 21, 129–173.

Olian, J. D., Carroll, S. J., & Giannantonio, C. M. (1993). Mentor reactions to protégés: An experiment with managers. *Journal of Vocational Behavior* 43, 266–278.

Olian, J. D., Carroll, S. J., Giannantonio, C. M., & Feren, D. B. (1988). What do protégés look for in a mentor? Results of three experimental studies. *Journal of Vocational Behavior* 33, 15–37.

O'Neil, J. M. & Wrightman, L. S. (2001). The mentoring relationship in psychology training programs. In S. Walfish & A. Hess (eds.) *Succeeding in graduate school: The complete career guide for the psychology student,* pp. 113–129. Hillsdale, NJ: Lawrence Erlbaum.

Pope, K. S. & Keith-Spiegel, P., & Tabachnick, B. G. (1986). Sexual attraction to clients: The human therapist and the (sometimes) inhuman training system. *American Psychologist* 41, 147–158.

Raabe, B. & Beehr, T. A. (2003). Formal mentoring versus supervisor and coworker relationships: Differences in perceptions and impact. *Journal of Organizational Behavior* 24, 271–293.

Ragins, B. R. (1997). Antecedents of diversified mentoring relationships. *Journal of Vocational Behavior* 51, 90–109.

Ragins, B. R. & Cotton, J. L. (1993). Gender and willingness to mentor in organizations. *Journal of Management* 19, 97–111.

Ragins, B. R. & Cotton, J. L. (1999) Mentor functions and outcomes: A comparison of men and women in formal and informal mentoring relationships. *Journal of Applied Psychology* 84, 529–550.

Ragins, B. R. & Scandura, T. A. (1994). Gender differences in expected outcomes of mentoring relationships. *Academy of Management Journal* 37, 957–971.

Roche, G. R. (1979). Much ado about mentors. *Harvard Business Review* 57, 14–28.

Rogers, C. R. (1961). *On becoming a person.* Boston: Houghton Mifflin.

Russell, J. E. A. & Adams, D. M. (1997). The changing nature of mentoring in organizations: An introduction to the special issues on mentoring and organizations. *Journal of Vocational Behavior* 51, 1–14.

Scandura, T. A. (1992). Mentorship and career mobility: An empirical investigation. *Journal of Organizational Behavior* 13, 169–174.

Scandura, T. A. & Ragins, B. R. (1993). The effects of sex and gender role orientation on mentorship in male-dominated occupations. *Journal of Vocational Behavior* 43, 251–265.

Schlosser, L. Z. & Gelso, C. J. (2001). Measuring the working alliance in advisor-advisee relationships in graduate school. *Journal of Counseling Psychology* 48, 157–167.

Scott, N. E. (1989). Differences in mentor relationships of non-white and white female professionals and organizational mobility: A review of the literature. *Psychology, A Journal of Human Behavior* 26, 23–26.

Silva, D. Y. & Tom, A. R. (2001). The moral basis of mentoring. *Teacher Education Quarterly* 28, 39–52.

Sosik, J. J. & Godshalk, V. M. (2000). Leadership styles, mentoring functions received, and job-related stress: A conceptual model and preliminary study. *Journal of Organizational Behavior* 21, 365–390.

Sternberg, R. J. (1995). Love as a story. *Journal of Social and Personal Relationships* 12, 541–546.

Strunk, W. & White, E. B. (2000). *The elements of style.* Boston: Allyn & Bacon.

Swap, W., Leonard, D., Shields, M., & Abrams, L. (2001). Using mentoring and storytelling to transfer knowledge in the workplace. *Journal of Management Information Systems* 18, 95–114.

Thomas, D. A. (1993). Racial dynamics in cross-race developmental relationships. *Administrative Science Quarterly* 38, 169–194.

Thomas, D. A. (2001). Race matters: The truth about mentoring minorities. *Harvard Business Review* 79, 99–107.

Turban, D. B. & Dougherty, T. W. (1994). Role of protégé personality in receipt of mentoring and career success. *Academy of Management Journal* 37, 688–702.

Whitely, W., Dougherty, T. W., & Dreher, G. F. (1991). Relationship of career mentoring and socioeconomic origins to managers' and professionals' early career success. *Academy of Management Journal* 34, 331–351.

Wright, C. A. & Wright, S. D. (1987). The role of mentors in the career development of young professionals. *Family Relations* 36, 204–208.

Zey, M. G. (1991). *The mentor connection: Strategic alliances in corporate life.* New Brunswick, NJ: Transaction Publishers.

Zuckerman, H. (1977). *Scientific elite: Nobel laureates in the United States.* New York: The Free Press.

Index